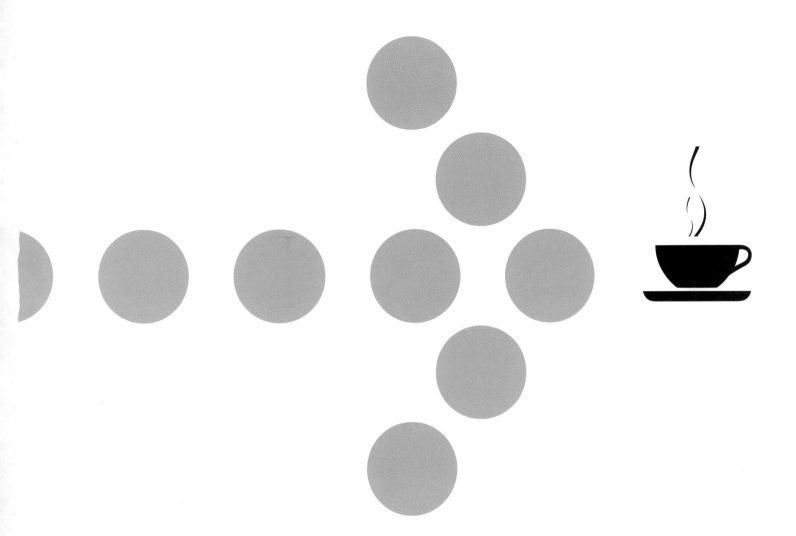

1,000

RESTAURANT BAR & CAFÉ GRAPHICS

From
Signage
to Logos
and Everything
in Between

LUKE HERRIOTT

ROCKPORT

BEVERLY MASSACHUSETTS

First published in the United States of America by Rockport Publishers, a member of Quayside Publishing Group
100 Cummings Center
Suite 406-L
Beverly, Massachusetts 01915
Telephone: (978) 282-9590, Fax: (978) 283-2742
www.rockpub.com

ISBN-13: 978-1-59253-332-9
ISBN-10: 1-59253-332-9

10 9 8 7 6 5 4 3 2 1

Design: Luke Herriott
Cover Design: Luke Herriott

Printed in China

ROCKPORT PUBLISHERS

1,000

RESTAURANT BAR & CAFÉ GRAPHICS

From Signage to Logos and Everything in Between

LUKE HERRIOTT

120 days

···➔

INTRODUCTION

The restaurant business is a risky and competitive world, and successful design is an essential component in an establishment's survival. A brand that has been cleverly designed portrays the style of a restaurant, bar, or café, helping to draw vital customers in. The work shown in **1,000 Restaurant, Bar, and Café Graphics** demonstrates how to create a concept that will direct and inform subtly and effectively.

A restaurant brand can suggest anything from a luxury dining experience to a cheap, cheerful snack. Successful branding influences who will enter, what they will order, how long they will stay, how much money they will part with, and most important, whether they will be a repeat customer.

This book is a feast of design concepts, showcasing 1,000 fresh ideas from some of the world's most successful and well-known designers. Featuring an international range of eating and drinking establishments, this book explores how brand identity can work its way into every aspect of a business, from its walls, door signs, and window graphics right down to its napkins, matchbooks, and tags.

Be informed and be inspired by what you see—and be sure to give your next project an extra bit of spice.

01.

00001–00174

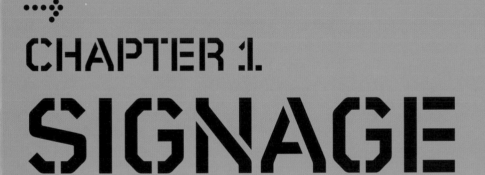

CHAPTER 1.
SIGNAGE

0001 ⋯⋗ Sea Design
      ⋯⋗ UK

0002 ⟶ Sea Design
⟶ UK

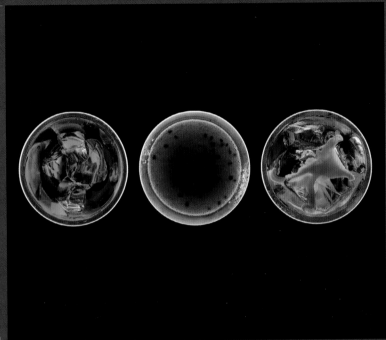

0003 ⟶ Sea Design
⟶ UK

0004 ⟶ i_d buero
⟶ Germany

0005 ⟶ i_d buero
⟶ Germany

0006 ⟶ Studio Output
⟶ UK

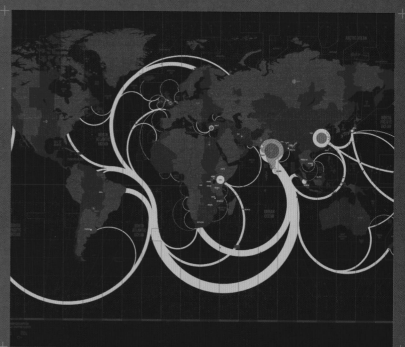

0007 ⟶ Studio Output
⟶ UK

0008 ⟶ Studio Output
⟶ UK

0009 ⟶ Studio Output
⟶ UK

001.1 ⇢ Willoughby Design Group
⇢ USA

0012 ···→ Hollis Brand Communications
···→ USA

0013 ···→ Willoughby Design Group
···→ USA

0014 ···→ Willoughby Design Group
···→ USA

0015 ···→ Willoughby Design Group
···→ USA

0016 ···→ Willoughby Design Group
···→ USA

0017 ···→ Willoughby Design Group
···→ USA

0018 ···→ Rome & Gold Creative
···→ USA

0019 ···→ Rome & Gold Creative
···→ USA

0020 ···→ Rome & Gold Creative
···→ USA

0021 ⇢ Rome & Gold Creative
  ⇢ USA

0022 ⇢ Rome & Gold Creative
  ⇢ USA

0023 ⇢ Rome & Gold Creative
  ⇢ USA

0024 ⇢ Rome & Gold Creative
  ⇢ USA

0027 ···⊳ Milton Glaser, Inc
···⊳ USA

0028 ···⊳ Milton Glaser, Inc
···⊳ USA

0029 ···⊳ Milton Glaser, Inc
···⊳ USA

0030 ···⊳ Milton Glaser, Inc
···⊳ USA

0031 ⟶ Studio Output
⟶ UK

0032 ⟶ Damion Hickman Design
⟶ USA

0033 ⟶ Hornall Anderson Design Works
⟶ USA

0034 ⟶ Elephant Design Pvt Ltd
⟶ India

0035 ⟶ Hornall Anderson Design Works
⟶ USA

0036 ⟶ Hornall Anderson Design Works
⟶ USA

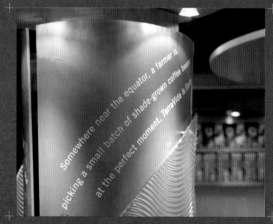

0037 ⟶ Hornall Anderson Design Works
⟶ USA

0038 ⟶ Hornall Anderson Design Works
⟶ USA

0039 ⟶ Hornall Anderson Design Works
⟶ USA

0042 ⤑ **sky design**
⤑ USA

0043 ⤑ Greiner Design Associates
⤑ USA

0044 ⤑ R&Mag Graphic Design
⤑ Italy

0045 ⤑ Greiner Design Associates
⤑ USA

0046 ⋯→ Hat Trick Design
⋯→ UK

0047 ⋯→ Hat Trick Design
⋯→ UK

0048 ⋯→ Hat Trick Design
⋯→ UK

0049 ⋯→ Frost Design, Sydney
⋯→ Australia

0052 ···> Fitch
···> USA

0053 ···> Fitch
···> USA

0054 ···> Walker Group
···> USA

0055 ···> Fitch
···> USA

0056 ···> Fitch
···> USA

0057 ···> Fitch
···> USA

0058 ···> Fitch
···> USA

0059 ···> Fitch
···> USA

0060 ···> Fitch
···> USA

0061 ⋯⊳ Brandhouse WTS
⋯⊳ UK

0062 ⋯⊳ christiansen: creative
⋯⊳ USA

0063 ⋯⊳ A1.0 Design
⋯⊳ Brazil

0064 ⋯⊳ A1.0 Design
⋯⊳ Brazil

53
FÜNFDREI

Love

to

take away™

parlour @ sketch

0067 ⋯⋗ Fitch
⋯⋗ USA

JavaCityCoffee

WHOLE BEAN OR CUSTOM GROUND

Fresh Roasted

DAILY

0068 ⋯⋗ The Dunlavey Studio
⋯⋗ USA

THE MART
Food Court

0066 ⋯⋗ Warm Rain Ltd
⋯⋗ UK

0069 ⋯⋗ Richard Poulin Design Group
⋯⋗ USA

0071 ⋯⇢ Walker Group
⋯⇢ USA

0072 ⋯⇢ Fitch
⋯⇢ USA

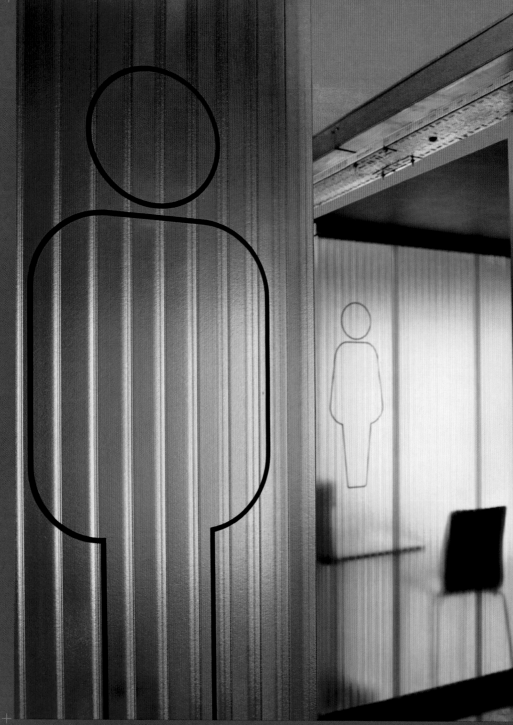

0075 ⋯→ **R&Mag Graphic Design**
⋯→ Italy

0076 ⋯→ **Elfen**
⋯→ Wales

0079 ⋯➔ Studio Output
⋯➔ UK

0080 ⋯➔ A1.0 Design
⋯➔ Brazil

0081 ⋯➔ Brandhouse WTS
⋯➔ UK

0082 ⋯➔ Brandhouse WTS
⋯➔ UK

0084 ··→ Vital Signs & Graphics
··→ USA

0085 ··→ Vital Signs & Graphics
··→ USA

0086 ··→ Hollis Brand Communications
··→ USA

0087 ⇢ i_d buero
⇢ Germany

0088 ⇢ Jonni
⇢ Norway

0089 ⇢ Kenneth Diseño
⇢ Mexico

0090 ⇢ Jonni
⇢ Norway

0091 ⇢ Pentagram Design
⇢ USA

0092 ⇢ Pentagram Design
⇢ USA

0093 ⇢ Poulin & Morris
⇢ USA

0094 ⇢ Crush Design & Art Direction
⇢ UK

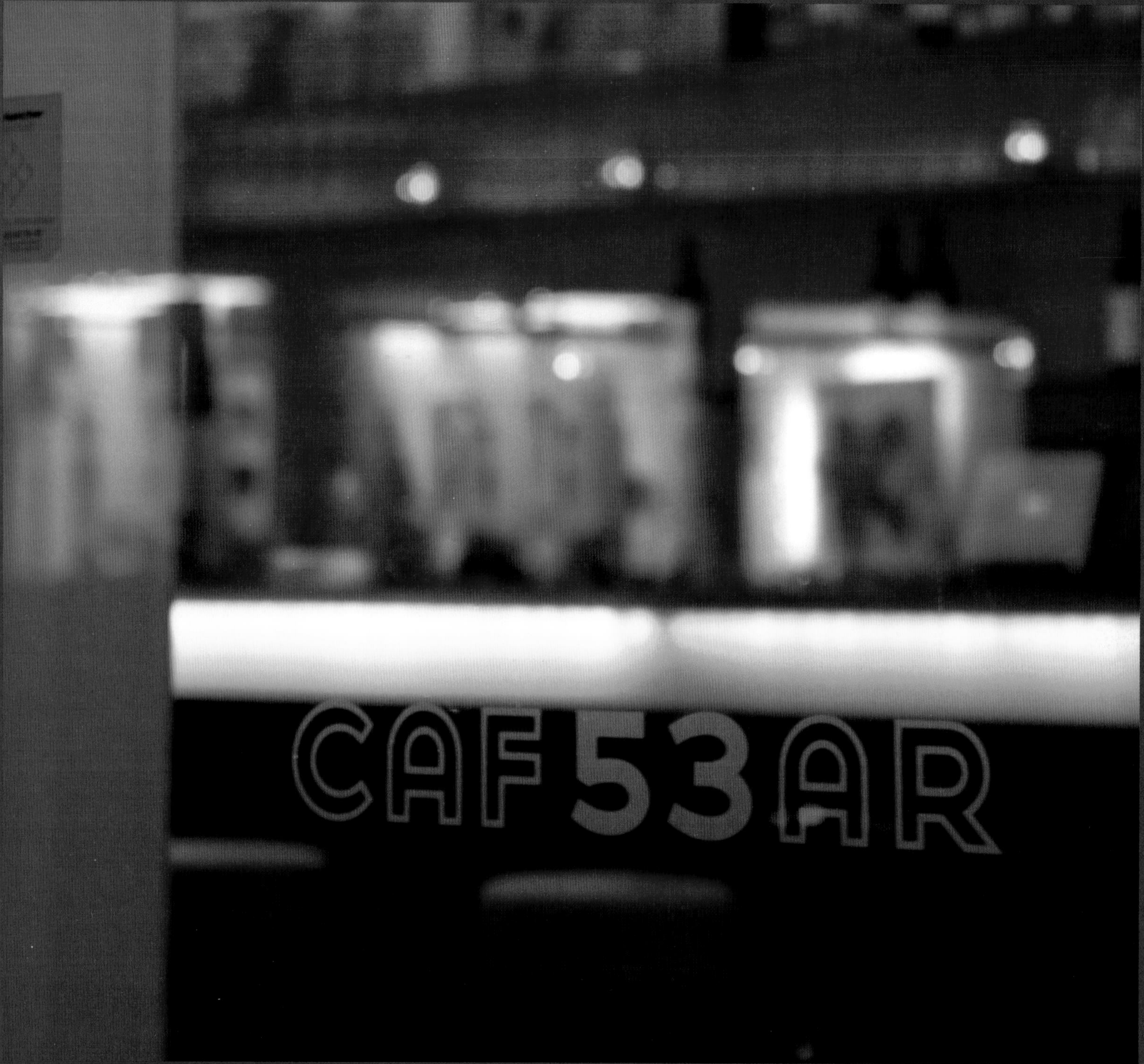

0095 Finest/Magma
Germany

0096 ⇢ Big Eyes Design
⇢ Israel

0097 ⇢ Big Eyes Design
⇢ Israel

0098 ⇢ Taxi Studio Ltd
⇢ UK

0099 ⇢ Taxi Studio Ltd
⇢ UK

0100 ⇢ AdamsMorioka
⇢ USA

0101 ⇢ AdamsMorioka
⇢ USA

0102 ⇢ bonbon london
⇢ UK

0103 ⇢ Elephant Design Pvt Ltd
⇢ India

0104 ⇢ bonbon london
⇢ UK

01.05 ⤑ christiansen: creative
      ⤑ USA

01.06 ⤑ Jonni
      ⤑ Norway

01.07 ⤑ Sea Design
      ⤑ UK

01.08 ⤑ Mimolimit
      ⤑ Czech Republic

01.1.1 ···→ Minelli, Inc
···→ USA

01.1.2 ···→ Minelli, Inc
···→ USA

01.1.3 ···→ i_d buero
···→ Germany

01.1.4 ···→ Vrontikis Design Office
···→ USA

.5 ⋯▸ AdamsMorioka
⋯▸ USA

01.16 ⋯▸ Hamagami/Carroll, Inc
⋯▸ USA

01.17 ⋯▸ Hamagami/Carroll, Inc
⋯▸ USA

01.18 ⋯▸ Hollis Brand Communications
⋯▸ USA

01.19 ⋯▸ Hamagami/Carroll, Inc
⋯▸ USA

01.20 ⋯▸ Hamagami/Carroll, Inc
⋯▸ USA

01.21 ⋯▸ Vrontikis Design Office
⋯▸ USA

01.22 ⋯▸ Vrontikis Design Office
⋯▸ USA

01.23 ⋯▸ The Dunlavey Studio
⋯▸ USA

01.24 ⟶ Hamagami/Carroll, Inc
⟶ USA

01.26 ⋯→ sky design
⋯→ USA

01.27 ⋯→ S&N Design
⋯→ USA

01.25 ⋯→ AdamsMorioka
⋯→ USA

01.28 ⋯→ Kenneth Diseño
⋯→ Mexico

01.29 ···➔ Mary Hutchinson LLC Design
···➔ USA

01.30 ···➔ Mirko Ilić Corp.
···➔ USA

01.31 ···➔ Mirko Ilić Corp.
···➔ USA

01.32 ···➔ Mirko Ilić Corp.
···➔ USA

01.33 ⋯⟶ R&Mag Graphic Design
  ⋯⟶ Italy

01.34 ⋯⟶ sky design
  ⋯⟶ USA

01.35 ···> sky design
···> USA

01.36 ⋯⟩ **Hollis Brand Communications**
⋯⟩ USA

01.37 ⋯⟩ **R&Mag Graphic Design**
⋯⟩ Italy

01.38 ⋯⟩ **Frost Design, Sydney**
⋯⟩ Australia

01.39 ⋯⟩ **R&Mag Graphic Design**
⋯⟩ Italy

01.40 ⋯⟩ **Hornall Anderson Design Works**
⋯⟩ USA

01.41 ⋯⟩ **Hornall Anderson Design Works**
⋯⟩ USA

01.42 ⋯⟩ **R&Mag Graphic Design**
⋯⟩ Italy

01.43 ⋯⟩ **Kenneth Diseño**
⋯⟩ Mexico

01.44 ⋯⟩ **Kenneth Diseño**
⋯⟩ Mexico

01.45 ⇢ bonbon london
⇢ UK

01.46 ⇢ Damion Hickman Design
⇢ USA

01.47 ⇢ Braue Strategic Brand Design
⇢ Germany

01.48 ⇢ Tharp Did It
⇢ USA

0149 ⟶ Elfen
⟶ Wales

0150 ⟶ Hollis Brand Communications
⟶ USA

01.52 ⇢ urban INFLUENCE design studio
⇢ USA

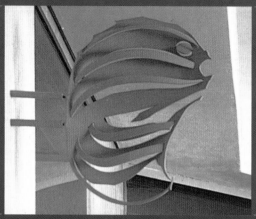

01.53 ⇢ Alexander Design Associates
⇢ USA

01.54 ⇢ Fullblastinc.com
⇢ USA

01.55 ⇢ Marve Cooper Design, Ltd.
⇢ USA

01.56 ⇢ Tharp Did It
⇢ USA

01.57 ⇢ Qually & Company
⇢ USA

01.58 ⇢ The Dunlavey Studio
⇢ USA

01.59 ⇢ The Dunlavey Studio
⇢ USA

01.60 ⇢ The Dunlavey Studio
⇢ USA

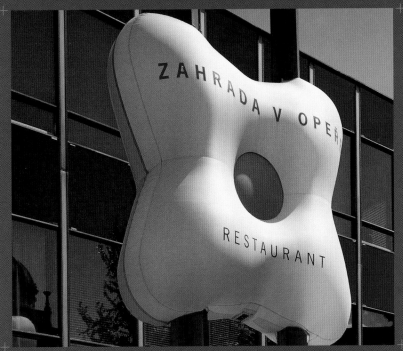

0161 ⋯➔ Hollis Brand Communications
⋯➔ USA

0162 ⋯➔ John Kneapler Design
⋯➔ USA

0163 ⋯➔ Mimolimit
⋯➔ Czech Republic

0164 ⋯➔ Hunt Weber Clark Associates
⋯➔ USA

0166 ⋯⋑ Evenson Design Group
⋯⋑ USA

0167 ⋯⋑ Pentagram Design
⋯⋑ USA

0168 ⋯⋑ Greteman Group
⋯⋑ USA

0169 ⋯⋑ The Invisions Group Ltd.
⋯⋑ USA

0170 ⋯⋑ Evenson Design Group
⋯⋑ USA

0171 ⋯⋑ The Art Commission, Inc.
⋯⋑ USA

0172 ⋯⋑ Sayles Graphic Design
⋯⋑ USA

0173 ⋯⋑ Les LaMotte Design
⋯⋑ USA

0174 ⋯⋑ Hunt Weber Clark Associates
⋯⋑ USA

01.75-03898 →

→

02

CHAPTER 2
LOGOS

BM

0176 ···❯ Studio Output
···❯ UK

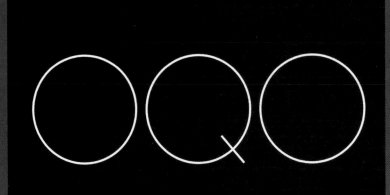

0177 ···❯ Studio Output
···❯ UK

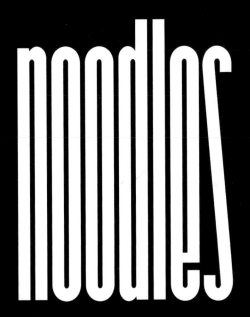

0178 ···❯ Mimolimit
···❯ Czech Republic

0179 ···❯ Sea Design
···❯ UK

01.80 ⇢ Etc Diseño Gráfico
  ⇢ Venezuela

01.81 ⇢ Unreal
  ⇢ UK

01.82 ⇢ Unreal
  ⇢ UK

01.83 ⇢ Jonni
  ⇢ Norway

Geisha

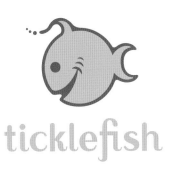

0187 ···> urban INFLUENCE design studio
···> USA

0188 ···> BigEyes Design
···> Israel

0189 ···> 28 Limited Brand
···> Germany

0190 ···> 28 Limited Brand
···> Germany

0191 ···> 28 Limited Brand
···> Germany

0192 ···> 28 Limited Brand
···> Germany

0193 ···> Commarts, Inc
···> USA

0194 The Jones Group
···> USA

01.95 → Turnstyle
→ USA

01.96 → Tom Varisco Designs
→ USA

01.97 → Kenneth Diseño
→ Mexico

01.98 → Graphicwise Inc
→ USA

BASS STREET

B

CHOP HOUSE

Rib Shack

Famous Barbecue

LUNCH & DINNER

0201 ⇢ The Jones Group
⇢ USA

0202 ⇢ Campus Collection
⇢ USA

LA POSADA

PARRILLA NORTEÑA
& CANTINA

0205 ⋯⟩ Advance Design Centre
⋯⟩ USA

0206 ⋯⟩ Jeff Fisher LogoMotives
⋯⟩ USA

0207 ⋯⟩ Advance Design Centre
⋯⟩ USA

0208 ⋯⟩ Advance Design Centre
⋯⟩ USA

0209 ⋯⟩ Hansen Associates
⋯⟩ USA

0210 ⋯⟩ Laguna College of Art & Design
⋯⟩ USA

0211 ⋯⟩ Jeff Fisher LogoMotives
⋯⟩ USA

0212 ⋯⟩ Strata-Media Inc
⋯⟩ USA

0213 ⋯⟩ BigEyes Design
⋯⟩ Israel

0216 ⋯⋗ Inaria
⋯⋗ UK

0217 ⋯⋗ Sayles Graphic Design
⋯⋗ USA

0218 ⋯⋗ R&Mag Graphic Design
⋯⋗ Italy

0219 ⋯⋗ AdamsMorioka
⋯⋗ USA

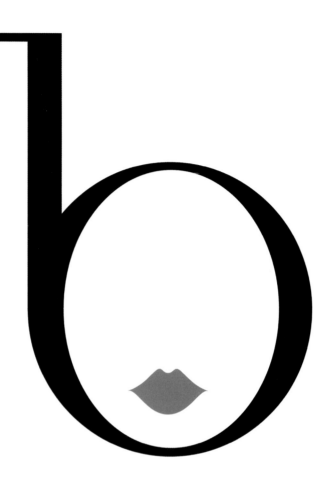

0220 ···▶ From Scratch Design Studio
···▶ USA

0221 ···▶ Dornig Graphic Design
···▶ Austria

THREE BELOW

0223 ⋯➜ Spark Studio Pty Ltd
⋯➜ Australia

0224 ⇢ Re-Public
⇢ Denmark

0225 ⇢ The Jones Group
⇢ USA

0226 ⇢ The Jones Group
⇢ USA

Legato

SpiNOUT

0227 ⇢ LM
⇢ UK

0228 ⇢ Vrontikis Design Office
⇢ USA

0229 ⇢ Raidy Printing Company SAL
⇢ Lebanon

0230 ⇢ Q
⇢ Germany

0231 ⇢ Art Institute of California
⇢ USA

0232 ⇢ Ph.D
⇢ USA

GOLDBRICK HSE.

blattgold
Bar & Restaurant

0233 ⇢ Taxi Studio Ltd
⇢ USA

0234 ⇢ Q
⇢ Germany

BLEU
GOURMET

0235 ⇢ LM
⇢ UK

0236 ⇢ CDI Studios
⇢ USA

0239 ⟶ Ultra Design
⟶ USA

0240 ⟶ Advance Design Centre
⟶ USA

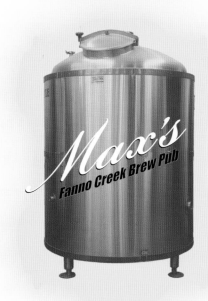

0241 ⟶ Fullblastinc.com
⟶ USA

0242 ⟶ Gingerbee Creative
⟶ USA

0243 ⋯→ Laguna College of Art & Design
⋯→ USA

0244 ⋯→ Prejean Creative
⋯→ USA

0245 ⋯→ Prejean Creative
⋯→ USA

0246 ⋯→ Prejean Creative
⋯→ USA

0247 ⋯→ Etc Diseño Gráfico
⋯→ Mexico

0248 ⋯→ Art Institute of California
⋯→ USA

0249 ⋯→ Crush Design & Art Direction
⋯→ USA

0250 ⋯→ VINE360
⋯→ USA

0251 ⋯→ BigEyes Design
⋯→ Israel

VINO VOYAGE

WINES TO MATCH YOUR MOOD

jillbartlett

CAFETERIA 124

Ladbroke Grove London W10

820

G O T H A M

FREDS 62

FOR BREAKFAST ALL DAY LONG

0258 ⋯⇨ Smart Works
    ⋯⇨ Australia

0259 ⋯⇨ Finest/Magma
    ⋯⇨ Germany

0260 ⋯⇨ Lodge Design
    ⋯⇨ USA

0261 ⋯⇨ Finest/Magma
    ⋯⇨ Germany

BAR > LOUNGE

0262 ⋯∗ Gabriel Kalach - Visual Communication
⋯∗ USA

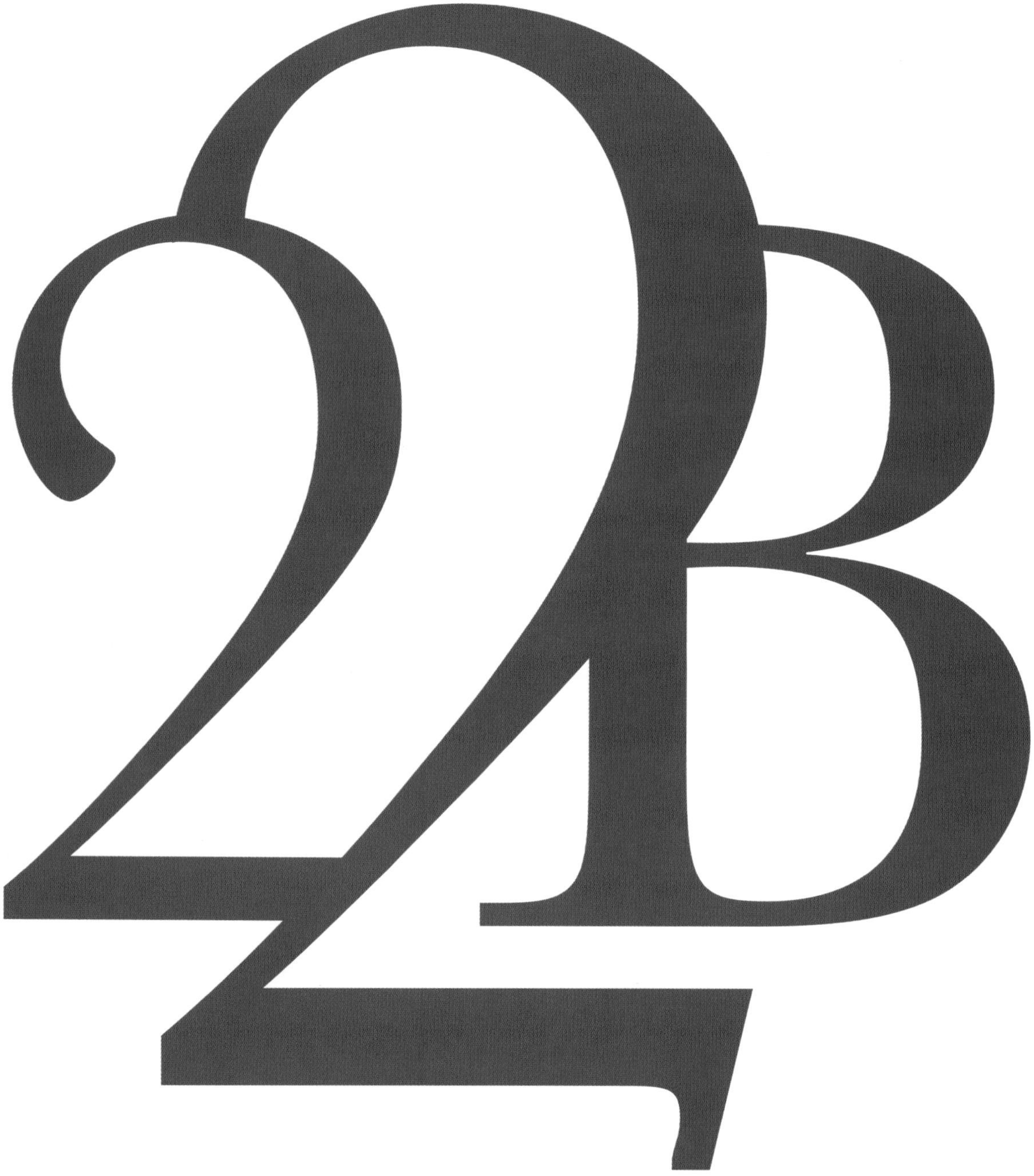

RASIKA
FLAVORS OF INDIA

0264 ⋯⟶ From Scratch Design Studio
⋯⟶ USA

GALARIE
IM DG HYP — WINTERGARTEN

0265 ⋯⟶ Ducks Design
⋯⟶ USA

ginza
Japanese restaurant

sushi bar
hibachi grill

0266 ⋯⟶ Restaurant Identity.com
⋯⟶ USA

La tartine

0267 ⋯⟶ Hand Made Group
⋯⟶ Italy

O'ASIAN
KITCHEN ✦ DIM SUM ✦ BAR

0268 ⋯⟶ Mary Hutchinson Design LLC
⋯⟶ USA

RESTAURANT
LeuchtFeuer

0269 ⋯⟶ Braue Strategic Brand Design
⋯⟶ Germany

titanic
luncheonette • caterer
445 st.pierre, montreal • tel. 849-0894

0270 ⋯⟶ Ducks Design
⋯⟶ USA

THE wine bar

0271 ⋯⟶ R&Mag Graphic Design
⋯⟶ Italy

REFLEX
LOUNGE · BAR

0272 ⋯⟶ Heinzle Design
⋯⟶ Austria

0273 ---> Finest/Magma
---> Germany

0274 ---> Finest/Magma
---> Germany

FOOD COLOSSEUM

0275 ---> Vrontikis Design Office
---> USA

0276 ---> Bowhaus Design Groupe
---> USA

≡ GelbeSeiten ®
BarCafeLounge

toulouse

SHIBUYA

0279 ⤏ Lorenza Zanni
⤏ Italy

0280 ⤏ Warm Rain Ltd
⤏ UK

DA VINCI'S

0283 ⋯⟩ Octavo Design Pty Ltd
⋯⟩ Australia

l'auberge

0284 ⋯⟩ Q
⋯⟩ Germany

MOJO'S
SPORTS BAR

0285 ⋯⟩ Prejean Creative
⋯⟩ USA

encounter
restaurant

0286 ⋯⟩ AdamsMorioka
⋯⟩ USA

BLUE ⋆ RIBBON
STEAK HOUSE
EST. 20 04

0287 ⋯⟩ Sayles Graphic Design
⋯⟩ USA

JAVA GOOD

0288 ⋯⟩ Sayles Graphic Design
⋯⟩ USA

Franco Latino

0289 ⋯⟩ Oliver Russell
⋯⟩ USA

TRAMONTO'S™
STEAK & SEAFOOD

0290 ⋯⟩ The Jones Group
⋯⟩ USA

Club ⋆ Luna

0291 ⋯⟩ Eye Speak
⋯⟩ USA

THE **PERKY PARROT**

0294 ···⟩ Commarts Inc
···⟩ USA

0295 ···⟩ Sayles Graphic Design
···⟩ USA

Vue de Monde

pieros
RESTAURANT & CLUB

indulge

VERVE

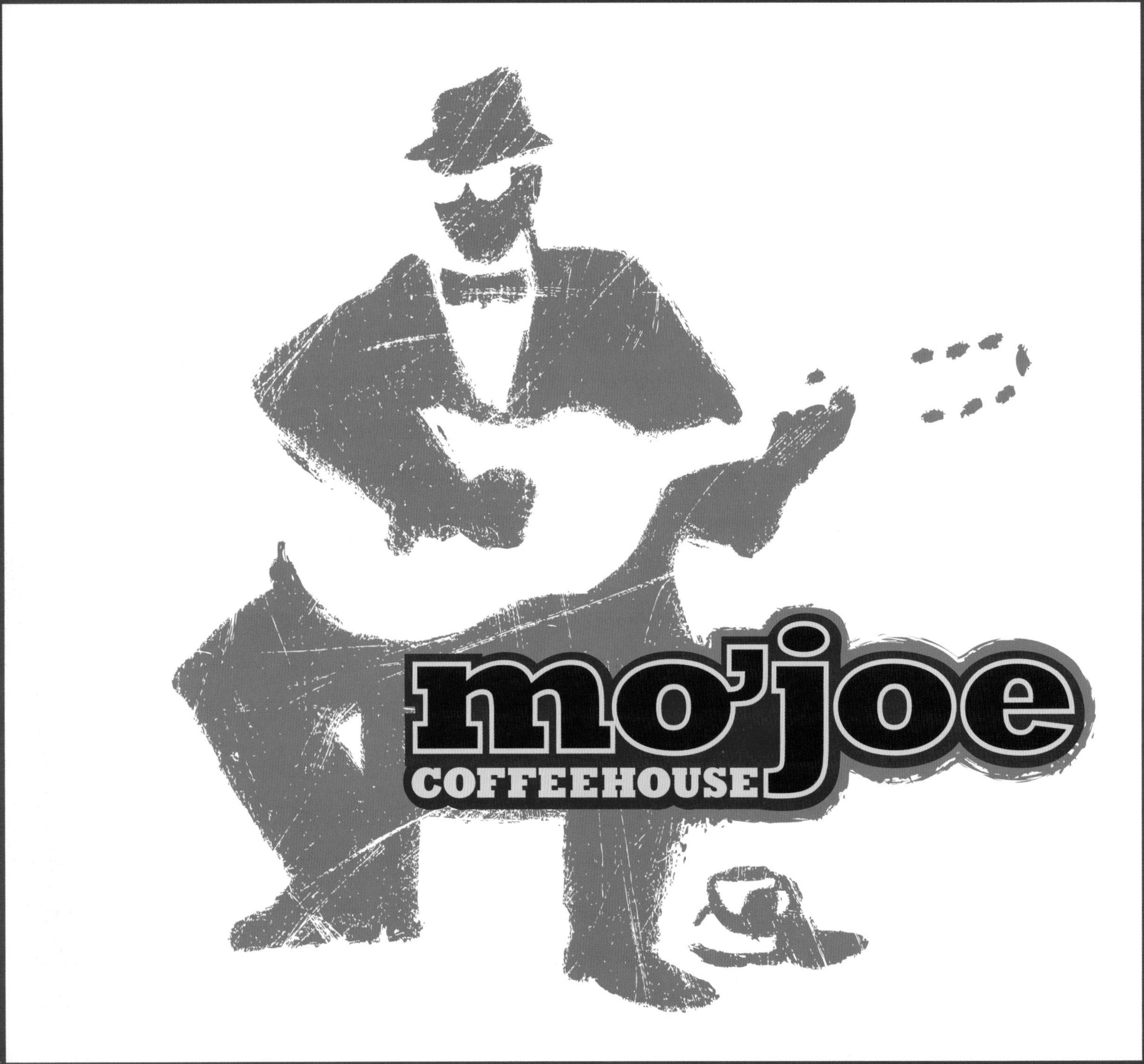

0303 → Dean Johnson Design
→ USA

0304 --> TD2, Identity & Strategic Design
--> Mexico

0305 --> Fresh Oil
--> USA

0306 --> Kenneth Diseño
--> Mexico

0307 --> Spark Communications Inc
--> USA

0308 --> Fresh Oil
--> USA

0309 --> Fresh Oil
--> USA

0310 --> Lodge Design Company
--> USA

0311 --> Gabriel Kalach - Visual Communication
--> USA

0312 --> Fresh Oil
--> USA

IT'S HIP TO BE SQUARE

BAR • RESTAURANT

0318 →∙ Gabriel Kalach - Visual Communication
→∙ USA

0319 → Mark Frankel Design, Inc
→ USA

0320 → Regan Blough
→ USA

0321 → Thielen Designs
→ USA

0322 → Thielen Designs
→ USA

0323 ⋯➔ Octavo Design Pty Ltd
⋯➔ Australia

0324 ⋯➔ CDI Studios
⋯➔ USA

0325 ⋯➔ CDI Studios
⋯➔ USA

0326 ⋯➔ The Jones Group
⋯➔ USA

0327 ⋯➔ The Jones Group
⋯➔ USA

MORTIMERS

0328 ⋯➔ Oliver Russell
⋯➔ USA

0329 ⋯➔ Mark Frankel Design Inc
⋯➔ USA

0330 ⋯➔ Vrontikis Design Office
⋯➔ USA

REALTO
XXVI.MMIII

0331 ⋯➔ Ducks Design
⋯➔ Germany

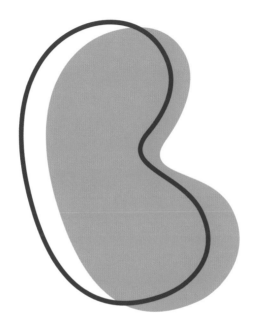

THE BEAN COUNTER

VEGGIE DELI & SOUP BAR

0334 ⇢ TD2, Identity & Strategic Design
⇢ Mexico

0335 ⇢ TD2, Identity & Strategic Design
⇢ Mexico

0336 ⇢ TD2, Identity & Strategic Design
⇢ Mexico

0337 ⇢ Damion Hickman Design
⇢ USA

0338 ⇢ Damion Hickman Design
⇢ USA

0339 ⇢ R&Mag Graphic Design
⇢ Italy

0340 ⇢ AdamsMorioka
⇢ USA

0341 ⇢ Campus Collection
⇢ USA

0342 ⇢ Campus Collection
⇢ USA

Décadence du Chocolat

0344 ···> Commarts Inc
···> USA

0345 ···> Vrontikis Design Office
···> USA

0346 ···> Kenneth Diseño
···> Mexico

0347 ···> R&Mag Graphic Design
···> Italy

0348 ···> Rome & Gold Creative
···> USA

0349 ···> David Caunce
···> UK

0350 ···> i_d buero
···> Germany

0351 ···> Fresh Oil
···> USA

0352 ···> Fresh Oil
···> USA

0353 ⋯→ **Ultra Design**
⋯→ USA

0354 ⋯→ **Ultra Design**
⋯→ USA

0355 ⋯→ **Ducks Design**
⋯→ Germany

0356 ⋯→ **Damion Hickman Design**
⋯→ USA

The BANK

CAFÉ BAR

0359 ⇢ Fresh Oil
⇢ USA

0360 ⇢ Rome & Gold Creative
⇢ USA

0361 ⇢ Restaurant Identity.com
⇢ USA

0362 ⇢ Restaurant Identity.com
⇢ USA

0363 ···⇢ Kenneth Diseño
···⇢ Mexico

0364 ···⇢ Kenneth Diseño
···⇢ Mexico

0365 ···⇢ Kenneth Diseño
···⇢ Mexico

0366 ···⇢ Kenneth Diseño
···⇢ Mexico

0367 ···⇢ Kenneth Diseño
···⇢ Mexico

0368 ···⇢ Kenneth Diseño
···⇢ Mexico

0369 ···⇢ Kenneth Diseño
···⇢ Mexico

0370 ···⇢ On The Edge Design, Inc
···⇢ USA

0371 ···⇢ bonbon london
···⇢ UK

0372 ⇢ Fresh Oil
  ⇢ USA

0373 ⇢ Vrontikis Design Office
  ⇢ USA

0374 ⇢ Kenneth Diseño
  ⇢ Mexico

0375 ⇢ Fresh Oil
  ⇢ USA

0376 ⇢ Fresh Oil
  ⇢ USA

0377 ⇢ Minelli Inc
  ⇢ USA

0378 ⇢ R&Mag Graphic Design
  ⇢ Italy

0379 ⇢ Ducks Design
  ⇢ Germany

0380 ⇢ Jeff Fisher LogoMotives
  ⇢ USA

THE
2005 COCK AND
TRUMPET

TOTTEM

0384 ⋯➤ Gabriel Kalach - Visual Communication
    ⋯➤ USA

0385 ⋯➤ Gabriel Kalach - Visual Communication
    ⋯➤ USA

WINE

D.O.C

BAR

WIRTSCHAFT ∗ZUR∗ SCHLACHT

∗SEMPACH∗

SMOKEJACK

• EST. 2004 •

BLUES & BARBEQUE

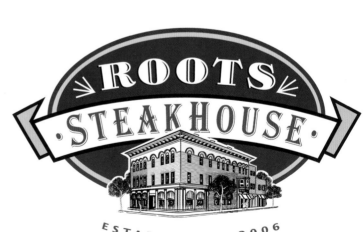

ROOTS

•STEAKHOUSE•

ESTABLISHED • 2006

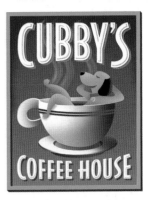

0390 --> Campus Collection
--> USA

0391 --> Braue Strategic Brand Design
--> Germany

0392 --> Evenson Design Group
--> USA

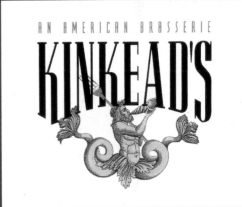

0393 --> Gabriel Kalach - Visual Communication
--> USA

0394 --> LM
--> UK

0395 --> The Invisions Group Ltd.
--> USA

0396 --> Rickabaugh Graphics
--> USA

0397 --> Evenson Design Group
--> USA

0398 --> Elephant Design, Pvt Ltd
--> India

03

→ →

03990-06990 →

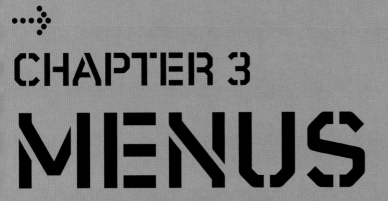

CHAPTER 3
MENUS

AFTERNOON TEA
Served from 2:30 pm to 5:00 pm
$18.00

POT OF TEA

TEA SANDWICHES
Smoked Salmon Napoleon
Cucumber and Watercress
Curried Chicken Salad with Granny Smith Apple
Warm Prosciutto and Fonti
Shrimp with Dill on Parmesan
Labneh (*kefir cheese*) on Markouk

SWEETS
Scone
Lemon Poppy Seed Cake
Chocolate Ganache Tart
Shortbread Cookies
Mocha Éclair
Carrot Cake

Preserve and Clotte

TEDDY BEAR TEA
Served from 2:30 to 5:00 pm
$14.00

KIDS BEVERAGES
Teddy's Tea Party
or
Hot Chocolate

and

Milk

CAFÉ OPALINE

0400 ⋯⇥ Minelli, Inc
⋯⇥ USA

0401 ⋯⇥ Taxi Studio Ltd
⋯⇥ UK

0402 ⋯⇥ i_d buero
⋯⇥ Germany

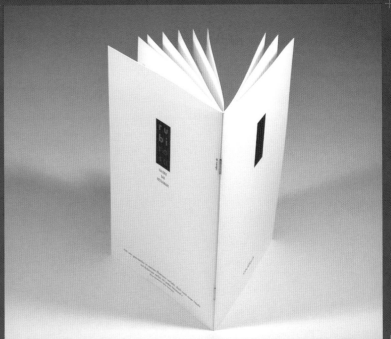

0403 ⋯⇥ i_d buero
⋯⇥ Germany

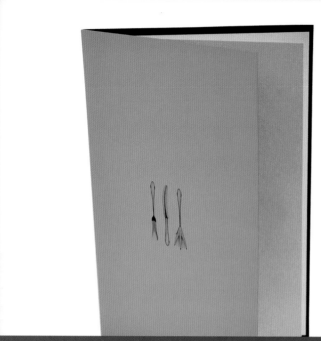

0404 ⋯▶ The Design Laboratory
⋯▶ UK

0405 ⋯▶ The Design Laboratory
⋯▶ UK

0406 ⋯▶ The Design Laboratory
⋯▶ UK

0407 ⋯▶ The Design Laboratory
⋯▶ UK

0409 ⋯› urban INFLUENCE design studio
⋯› USA

0410 ⋯› urban INFLUENCE design studio
⋯› USA

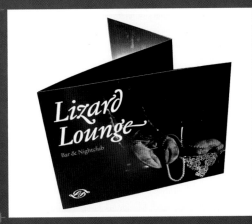

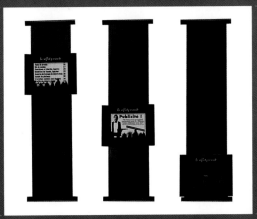

0411 ··→ Studio Output
··→ UK

0412 ··→ bonbon london
··→ UK

0413 ··→ Fabrice Praeger
··→ France

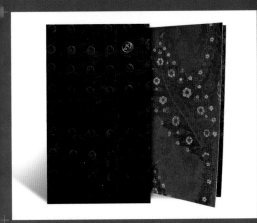

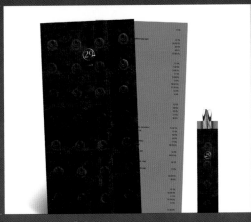

0414 ··→ Ayse Çelem
··→ Turkey

0415 ··→ Ayse Çelem
··→ Turkey

0416 ··→ Ayse Çelem
··→ Turkey

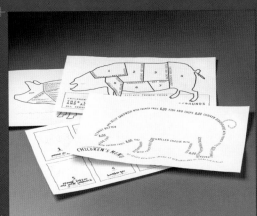

0417 ··→ Mirko Ilić Corp.
··→ USA

0418 ··→ STRONGtype
··→ USA

0419 ··→ bonbon london
··→ UK

0420 ⇢ 804© Graphic Design
     ⇢ Germany

0421 ⇢ Jonni
     ⇢ Norway

0422 ⇢ biz-R
     ⇢ UK

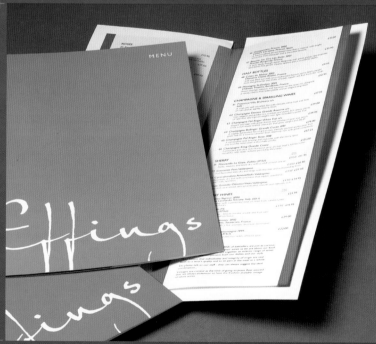

0423 ⇢ biz-R
     ⇢ UK

FOOD & DRINKS LIST

0426 ⇢ Crush Design & Art Direction
⇢ UK

0427 ⇢ Crush Design & Art Direction
⇢ UK

0428 ⇢ Morrow McKenzie Design
⇢ USA

0429 ⇢ Lodge Design Company
⇢ USA

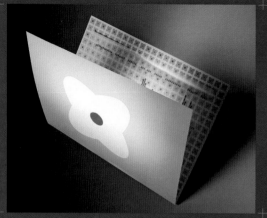

0430 ⇢ Mimolimit
⇢ Czech Republic

0431 ⇢ Mimolimit
⇢ Czech Republic

0432 ⇢ AdamsMorioka
⇢ USA

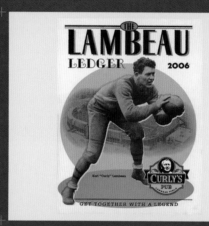

0433 ⇢ The Menu Workshop
⇢ USA

0434 ⇢ Mark Frankel Design, Inc
⇢ USA

0435 ⇢ Finest/Magma
⇢ Germany

0436 ⇢ LM
⇢ UK

0437 ⇢ Mark Frankel Design, Inc
⇢ USA

0438 ⇢ Rickabaugh Graphics
⇢ USA

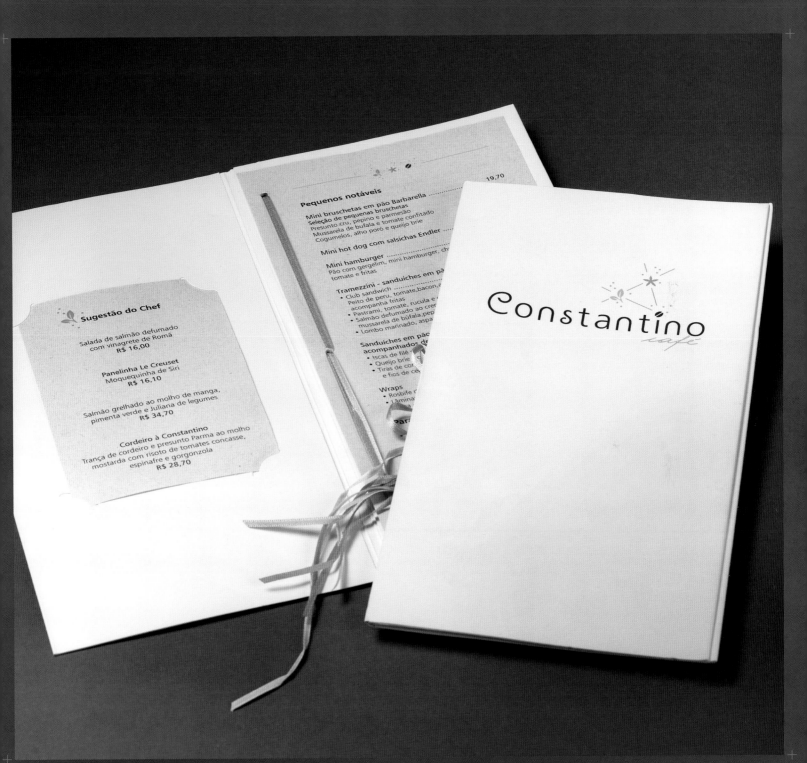

Sugestão do Chef

Salada de salmão defumado
com vinagrete de Romã
R$ 16,00

Panelinha Le Creuset
Moquequinha de Siri
R$ 16,10

Salmão grelhado ao molho de manga,
pimenta verde e Juliana de legumes
R$ 34,70

Cordeiro à Constantino
Trança de cordeiro e presunto Parma ao molho
mostarda com risoto de tomates concasse,
espinafre e gorgonzola
R$ 28,70

19,70

Pequenos notáveis

Mini bruschetas em pão Barbarella ....
Seleção de pequenas bruschetas
Presunto cru, pepino e parmesão
Mussarela de búfala e tomate confitado
Cogumelos, alho poró e queijo brie

Mini hot dog com salsichas Endler ....

Mini hamburger
Pão com gergelim, mini hamburger, ch
tomate e fritas

Tramezzini - sanduíches em pa
• Club sandwich
  Peito de peru, tomate,bacon,
  acompanha fritas
• Pastrami, tomate, rucula e
• Salmão defumado ao crem
  mussarela de búfala,pep
• Lombo marinado, aspa

Sanduíches em pão
acompanhados de
• Iscas de filé
• Queijo brie
• Tiras de co
  e fios de ce

Wraps
• Rosbife
• Lâmina

Para

Constantíno
café

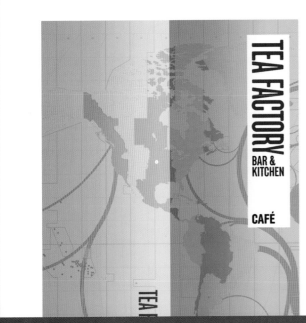

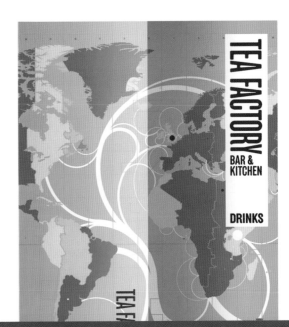

0441 ···› Studio Output
···› UK

0442 ···› Studio Output
···› UK

0443 ···› Threefold
···› Australia

0444 ···› Spark Studios Pty Ltd
···› Australia

0445 ⇢ Loewy
    ⇢ UK

0446 ⇢ Loewy
    ⇢ UK

0447 ⇢ Loewy
    ⇢ UK

0448 ⇢ Loewy
    ⇢ UK

Come out and play.

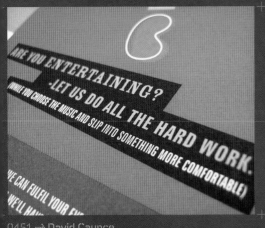

0451 ⇢ David Caunce
⇢ UK

0452 ⇢ David Caunce
⇢ UK

0453 ⇢ David Caunce
⇢ UK

0454 ⇢ David Caunce
⇢ UK

0455 ⇢ David Caunce
⇢ UK

0456 ⇢ Mirko Ilić Corp.
⇢ USA

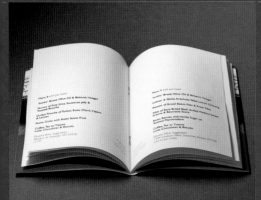

0457 ⇢ bonbon london
⇢ UK

0458 ⇢ bonbon london
⇢ UK

0459 ⇢ bonbon london
⇢ UK

0460 ⇢ Public
⇢ USA

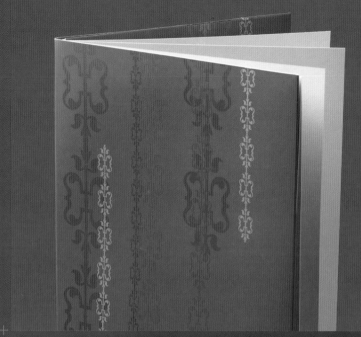

0461 ⇢ Public
⇢ USA

0462 ⇢ Public
⇢ USA

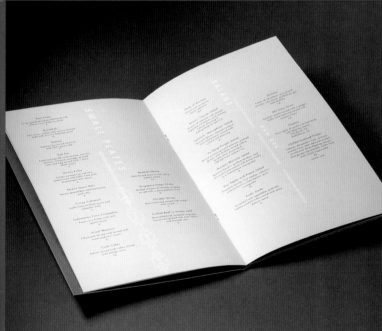

0463 ⇢ Public
⇢ USA

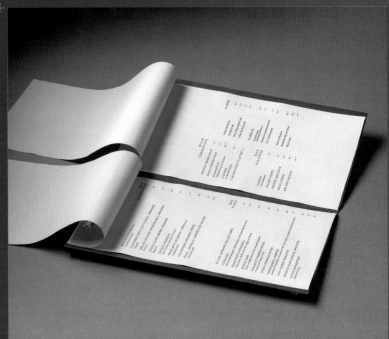

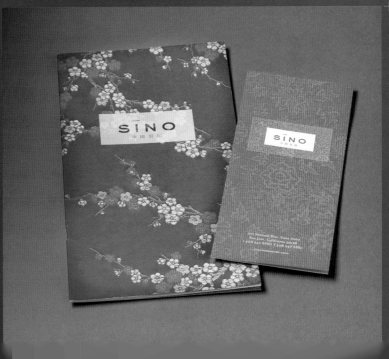

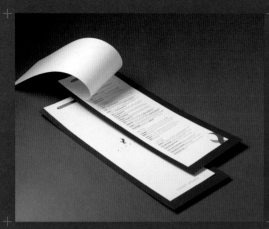

0470 ⇢ christiansen: creative
    ⇢ USA

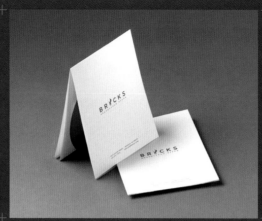

0471 ⇢ christiansen: creative
    ⇢ USA

0472 ⇢ 804© Graphic Design
    ⇢ Germany

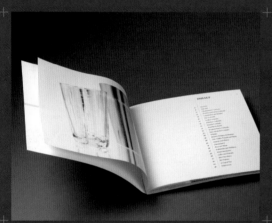

0473 ⇢ 804© Graphic Design
    ⇢ Germany

0474 ⇢ 804© Graphic Design
    ⇢ Germany

0475 ⇢ 804© Graphic Design
    ⇢ Germany

0476 ⇢ Bakken Creative Company
    ⇢ USA

0477 ⇢ BASELINE
    ⇢ Scotland

0478 ⇢ From Scratch Design Studio
    ⇢ USA

DIM SUM

¹ CHICKEN & MUSHROOM DUMPLING — 3
steamed open dumpling
dark meat, shrimp and shiitake mushroom
in an egg and flour (wonton skin) wrapper

² CHAR SIU BAO (char shoe bow) — 3
steamed white fluffy pork bun
bbq pork, oyster sauce, soy sauce and sugar
in a cornstarch and cake flour bun

³ VEGETARIAN DUMPLING — 3
steamed dumpling
bamboo shoots, water chestnuts, carrot
and shiitake mushroom in a rice flour wrapper

⁴ PAI GUAT (pie kwat) — plate
steamed pork sparerib
bone in sparerib with black beans and chili

⁵ CHICKEN FEET — plate
deep fried then steamed whole feet
chicken feet with oyster sauce

⁶ BEEF BALL — 3
steamed beef ball
ground beef, pork fat, onion
and water chestnut in a flour wrapper

3.75

⁷ EGG CUSTARD BUN — 3
steamed white fluffy bun filled with sweet egg
sweetened egg yolk, cream, butter, coconut juice
in a cake flour and baking powder bun

⁸ STEAMED LOTUS PASTE BUN — 3
steamed white fluffy bun filled with lotus paste
lotus paste and sugar

⁹ TARO PUFF — 3
fried taro dumpling with crispy coating
taro root, ground pork, shiitake mushroom,
dried shrimp, bbq pork and rice flour

¹⁰ SPRING ROLL — 3
classic vegetarian deep fried egg roll
with sweet and sour sauce, carrot, celery, glass noodle
in a rice flour wrapper

¹¹ GLUTINOUS RICE PUFF — 3
crispy hollow dumpling deep fried
sweet rice flour, ground pork, shiitake mushroom,
dried shrimp and bbq pork in rice flour wrapper

¹² POTSTICKER — 3
classic pork dumpling steamed and pan fried
ground pork, napa cabbage and ginger
in cake flour wrapper

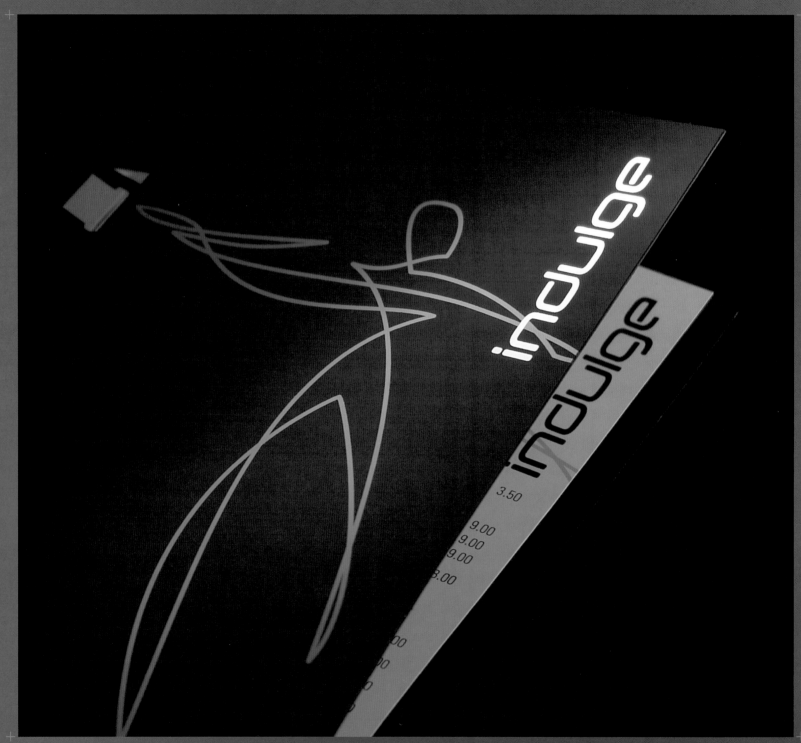

0481 ⋯→ AdamsMorioka
⋯→ USA

0482 ⋯→ Graphic Content
⋯→ USA

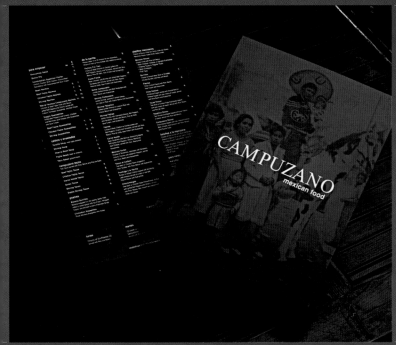

0483 ⋯→ Graphic Content
⋯→ USA

0484 ⋯→ Octavo Design Pty Ltd
⋯→ Australia

3 breakfasts at the 120 days

143 choices at the 120 days

Tapas

01 5 druhů tapasu podávaných s domací Focaccia
5 kinds of tapas served with home made Focaccia
160 Kč — 6,40 €

02 Košík chleba nebo Foccacia
Bread basket or Foccacia
35 Kč — 1,40 €

Polévka
Soup

03 Smetanová houbová polévka
Creamy mushroom soup
110 Kč — 4,40 €

04 Gaspaccio studená polévka
Gaspaccio cold soup
90 Kč — 3,60 €

Předkrmy
Starters

05 Hovězí Carpaccio s rukolou a hruškami
Beef carpaccio with pears, rocket leaves
and balsamic
180 Kč — 7,20 €

06 Sušené hovězí carpaccio
Dried beef carpaccio
310 Kč — 12,40 €

07 Sýrový talíř
French cheese plate
150 Kč — 6,00 €

08 Meloun s feta sýrem
Watermelon with feta cheese
110 Kč — 4,40 €

09 Italský talíř
Italian plate
230 Kč — 9,20 €

10 Křupavé kalamáry s mořskou solí a chilli
Crispy calamari with rock salt and chilli
165 Kč — 6,60 €

Hlavní jídla
Main courses

11 Club burger se slaninou, sýrem čedar, rajčaty
a hlávkovým salátem
Club burger with bacon, cheddar,
tomatoes and lettuce
240 Kč — 9,60 €

12 Francouzský burger s restovanou foie gras
a grilovanými houbami
French burger served with seared foie gras
and grilled mushrooms
290 Kč — 11,60 €

13 Kuřecí křidýlka s karamelovou chilli omáčkou
Chicken wings with chilli-caramel sauce
130 Kč — 5,20 €

14 Nabídka z křupavých Dim-Sum
se sladkou chilli omáčkou
Assortment of crispy Dim-Sum
with sweet chilli sauce
155 Kč — 6,20 €

Dezerty
Desserts

15 Tvarohový dort „New York style"
N.Y. style cheesecake
110 Kč — 4,40 €

16 Kokosové tiramisu
Coconut tiramisu
125 Kč — 5 €

17 Horký čokoládový dort
Hot chocolate cake
125 Kč — 5 €

18 Banana loty
Thai banana pancake
110 Kč — 4,40 €

19 Ovocný talíř
Fruits plate
120 Kč — 4,80 €

20 Variace zmrzliny
Variation of ice cream
80 Kč — 3,20 €

Děkujeme Vám za návštěvu restaurace **120 days**.
Thank you for visiting restaurant 120 days.

47 nights at the 120 days

70 wines at the 120 days

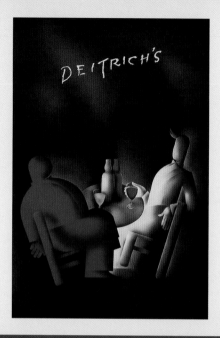

0489 ⇢ McCord Graphic Design
⇢ Country unavailable

0490 ⇢ Val Gene Associates
⇢ USA

0491 ⇢ From Scratch Design Studio
⇢ USA

0492 ⇢ Brandhouse WTS
⇢ UK

VINO
VOYAGE
WINES TO MATCH YOUR MOOD

ALL·BAR·ONE

INTRODUCTION
ADVENTUROUS
RELAXED
SOCIABLE
REFINED
PASSIONATE

Try new grapes, visit new places in the knowledge that with
All Bar One you're in safe hands. Bored of the usual,
try something different.

...classics

175ml   Bottle
...LLEY
...al Valley,
...ealand
...175 ml
...a satellite basin? Rich, ripe fruit
...a long soft dry finish

Red

HELL FIRE BAY   175ml   Bottle
Plantagenet,
Western Australia   4.00   16.00
Shiraz Grenache 14.5% abv
Energetic and spicy plum flavours

...CRAB
...berg,
...Australia
...Viognier 13% abv
...with a hint of fruit
...something unusual

17.50

FRESCOBALDI
POMINO ROSSO
Toscana,   24.50
Italy
Pinot Nair Sangiovese 2001 12.5% abv
Layers of red berry and a smooth
velvety feel

4.10   16.50

ADVENTUROUS
ADVENTUROUS
RELAXED
SOCIABLE
REFINED
PASSIONATE
YOUR FULL WINE LIST

0495 ⇢ BigEyes Design
　　⇢ USA

0496 ⇢ BigEyes Design
　　⇢ USA

0497 ⇢ BigEyes Design
　　⇢ USA

coffeeBAR
קפה · בר · מסעדה
יד חרוצים 13 · תל אביב
Delivery & TakeAway
688·9696
צהריים

coffeeBAR
קפה · בר · מסעדה
יד חרוצים 13 · תל אביב
Delivery & TakeAway
688·9696
ערב

Dessert Menu

PORT & SHERRY
By the Glass

DESSERT WINES

0498 ⇢ BigEyes Design
　　⇢ USA

0499 ⇢ BigEyes Design
　　⇢ USA

0500 ⇢ BigEyes Design
　　⇢ USA

NewYear Night 31.12.05

Champagne & Sparklin
White
Red
Dessert
Wine Special

NewYear Night 31.12.05

PORT & SHERRY
By the Glass

Sandeman	27	סנדמן
Sandeman Sherry Don Fino	30	סנדמן שרי דון פינו
Fonesca Bin 27	34	פונסקה בין 27
Fonesca Vintage 86	60	פונסקה וינטאג' 86
Otima	29	אוטימה
Tio Pepe Sherry	28	טיו פפה שרי
Drysack Oloroso 15	33	אלדרוסו 15
Don Guido Pedro Ximenez 20	33	פדרו חימנז 20
Jalifa Amontillado 30	38	אמונטיאדו 30
Pineau des Charentes	25	פינו דה שאראנט

0501 ⇢ BigEyes Design
　　⇢ USA

0502 ⇢ BigEyes Design
　　⇢ USA

0503 ⇢ BigEyes Design
　　⇢ USA

0504 ⋯▶ Allies
⋯▶ UK

0505 ⋯▶ Allies
⋯▶ UK

0506 ⋯▶ Allies
⋯▶ UK

0507 ⋯▶ Allies
⋯▶ UK

Banana
Almond
Coconut
Chocolate
Cantaloupe
Cappuccino

Ginger
Honey
Honeydew
Iced Coffee
Heath Mocha
French Vanilla

Mango
Lychee
Milk Tea
Lavender
Kona Mocha
Longan Honey

Sip it up™

BOBA TEA
COMPANY

"hotties"™

0510 ···› Rome & Gold Creative
      ···› USA

0511 ···› Brandhouse WTS
      ···› UK

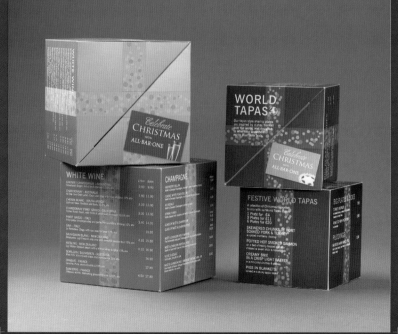

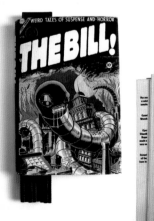

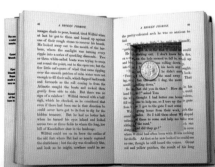

0512 ···› Brandhouse WTS
      ···› UK

0513 ···› Brandhouse WTS
      ···› UK

0514 ⟶ A1.0 Design
⟶ Brazil

0515 ⟶ A1.0 Design
⟶ Brazil

0516 ⟶ R&Mag Graphic Design
⟶ Italy

0517 ⟶ Hollis Brand Communication
⟶ USA

0518 ⟶ Associates Design
⟶ USA

0519 ⟶ Braue Strategic Brand Design
⟶ Germany

0520 ⟶ bonbon london
⟶ UK

0521 ⟶ Hardy Design
⟶ Italy

0522 ⟶ Braue Strategic Brand Design
⟶ Germany

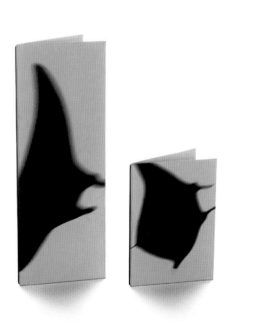

0529 → Fullblastinc.com
→ USA

0530 → Fullblastinc.com
→ USA

0531 → Brandhouse WTS
→ UK

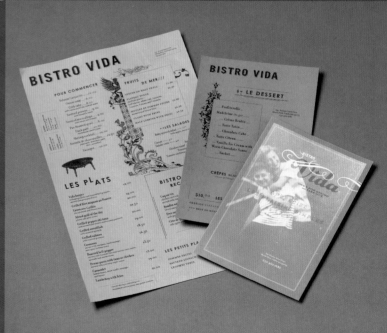

0532 → Public
→ USA

BRASSERIE

M&R

DELIVERY & TAKEAWAY

א'-ה' 12:00-16:00, 19:00-חצות • שישי 19:00-חצות • שבת 13:00-חצות

בראסרי שרות משלוחים

LES SALADES

38	סלט ניסואז עם טונה בשמן זית, פלפלים ואנשובי
36	סלט אנדיב, רוקפור ואגוזי לוז
28	לבבות חסה ערבית וביקון ביניגרט שמפניה
16	סלט עגבניות, כוסברה ובצל אדום
28	סלט עלי סלק ומוצרלה עם סלק קלוי, שמן זית ולימון
32	סלט יווני עם פלפלים, מלפפונים, עגבניות וגבינת פטה

ENTRéES

18	מרק היום
22	מרק עוף עם אטריות
28	פטה כפרי
36	רביולי במילוי סרטנים עם עגבניות קלויות ואספרגוס

PLATS PRINCIPAUX

Side Dishes

18	צ'יפס
16	ירק מאודה
14	אורז יסמין
12	סלט ירוק

48	חזה עוף במרינדה של חרדל וסויה, עשוי בגריל
38	שניצל עוף
58	חצי עוף צלוי בטרגון וראשי שום אפויים
72	צלע חזיר בגריל, בסויה, צ'ילי ודבש
48	מרגז בגריל עם סלט עגבניות
42/38	המבורגר אמריקאי 220 גר' / 300 גר'
48/44	- עם גבינת אמנטל
38	ירקות מאודים

בימי חול בצהריים (12:00-16:00) כל המנות העיקריות והסנדוויצ'ים
מוגשים עם מנה ראשונה לבחירתכם - סלט ירוק עם פירות ואגוזים או מרק

SANDWICHES

Pasta

Desserts

28

עוגת שוקולד
תותים בשמנת (בעונה)
מוס שוקולד
קרם שניט
טארט אגסים/שזיפים

0535 ⇢ AdamsMorioka
⇢ USA

0536 ⇢ BigEyes Design
⇢ Israel

0537 ⇢ BigEyes Design
⇢ Israel

0538 ⇢ BigEyes Design
⇢ Israel

0539 ⇢ BigEyes Design
⇢ Israel

0540 ⇢ Fresh Oil
⇢ USA

0541 ⇢ Finest/Magma
⇢ Germany

0542 ⇢ BigEyes Design
⇢ Israel

0543 ⇢ Fresh Oil
⇢ USA

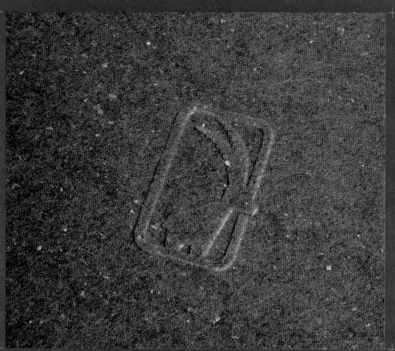

0544 ⋯⇥ **Ducks Design**
⋯⇥ Germany

0545 ⋯⇥ **Ducks Design**
⋯⇥ Germany

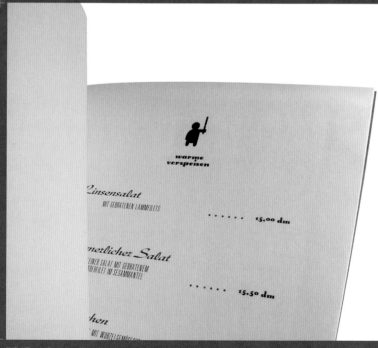

0546 ⋯⇥ **Restaurant Identity.com**
⋯⇥ USA

0547 ⋯⇥ **Ducks Design**
⋯⇥ Germany

Treat DNA

Our Taste Specialists have been working hard to map the variety of flavors available at Sheridan's. Now you can mix up your favorite flavors for your own unique Treat DNA.

 CAKE BATTER
 SUGAR FREE
 BLACK BERRY
 FOAM
 TRUFFLE
 BANANA
 BROWNIE
 PIE
 PUMPKIN PIE

 DREAMSICLE
 REESE'S PIECES®
 GRAHAM CRACKER
 CONE
 HOT DRINKS
 FAVORITE TOPPING
 WOWIECCINO
 HAZELNUT
 BEVERAGE

 TOFFEE
 COOKIE DOUGH
 BUNDT CAKE
 CONCRETE
 M&M'S®
 CHOCOLATE
 REESE'S®
 COTTON CANDY
 LATTÉ

 LEMON
 APPLE PIE
 IRISH CREME
 ALMOND
 PINEAPPLE
 HOT DOG
 ON ICE
 RICE KRISPIES®
 OREO®

 WHIPPED CREAM
 CARAMEL
 PRETZEL
 CHERRY
 MILK
 MINT
 PEANUT BUTTER
 MARSH MALLOW
 ESPRESSO

0550 --> Hollis Brand Communications
--> USA

0551 --> Willoughby Design Group
--> USA

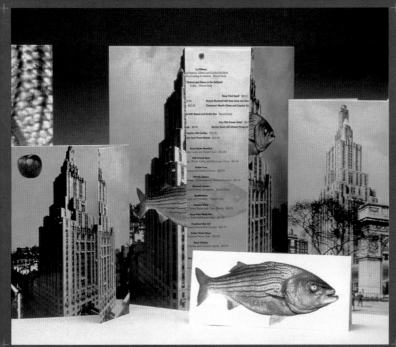

0552 --> Pentagram Design
--> USA

0553 --> Hornall Anderson Design Works
--> USA

0554 →› Disney Design Group
→› USA

0555 →› christiansen: creative
→› USA

0556 →› Fullblastinc.com
→› USA

0557 →› On The Edge Design, Inc
→› USA

0558 →› On The Edge Design, Inc
→› USA

0559 →› Associates Design
→› USA

0560 →› Associates Design
→› USA

0561 →› Lance Anderson Design
→› USA

0562 →› John & Orna Designs
→› UK

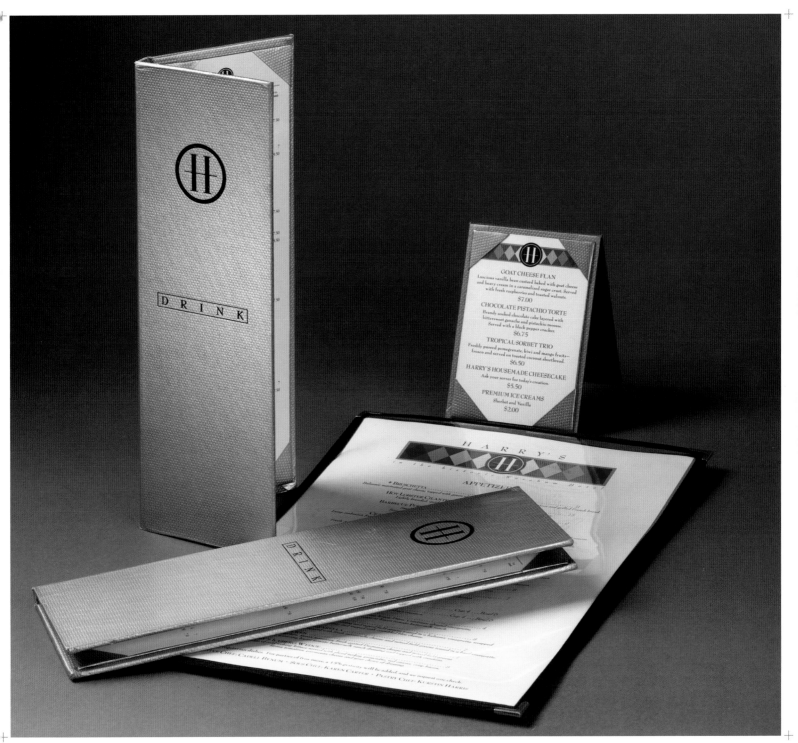

APPETIZERS

BAKED BRIE EN CROUTE
Baked Brie in puff pastry served with fresh fruit.
5.95

ESCARGOT CHAMPIGNON
Sautéed with garlic and wild mushrooms in a rich Bordelaise sauce; served atop puff pastry.
6.25

SHRIMP COCKTAIL
Large Gulf shrimp served with cocktail sauce and lemon.
7.95

MEDITERRANEAN ONION SOUP
Italian tomato and onion soup.
3.50

SOUP OF THE DAY
Made fresh daily.
3.50

SALADS

EAGLE'S NEST CHICKEN SALAD
Garnished with tomato, egg, fresh fruit, nutbread, and sherbet.
7.95

SALAD NIÇOISE
Albacore tuna, hearts of palm, new potatoes, and black olives; served with Caesar dressing.
7.95

SEAFOOD PASTA SALAD
Fettuccine verde with shrimp, scallops, and mussels tossed with vinaigrette.
7.95

ENTRÉES

BROCHETTE OF BEEF
Medallions of tender beef with grilled vegetables.
7.95

PEPPER SEARED SWORDFISH
Fresh swordfish basted with green peppercorns in a red wine sauce.
7.95

EAGLE'S NEST CLUB
Shaved ham and turkey, crisp bacon, lettuce, onion, and tomato.
5.95

SHRIMP CARBONARA
Marinated shrimp with bacon and peas in an Alfredo cream sauce served atop angel hair pasta.
7.95

BLACK FOREST SANDWICH
Grilled onions with prime rib, Swiss cheese, and Thousand Island dressing on honey nut bread.
7.95

CHICKEN STIR-FRY
Sautéed chicken with oriental vegetables and teriyaki sauce; served atop lemon-pepper angel hair pasta.
7.95

GRILLED SALMON
A fresh fillet grilled and served with cucumber dill sauce.
7.95

LEMON CHICKEN WITH CAPER, PINE NUT SAUCE
Grilled chicken topped with a light sauce of capers and roasted pine nuts.
6.95

ROASTED PRIME RIB OF BEEF
Slow roasted and sliced to order, our prime rib may also be blackened.
8.95

0565 ⇢ Mary Hutchinson Design LLC
⇢ USA

0566 ⇢ Val Gene Associates
⇢ USA

0567 ⇢ Val Gene Associates
⇢ USA

0568 ⇢ Val Gene Associates
⇢ USA

0569 ⇢ John & Orna Designs
    ⇢ UK

0570 ⇢ John & Orna Designs
    ⇢ UK

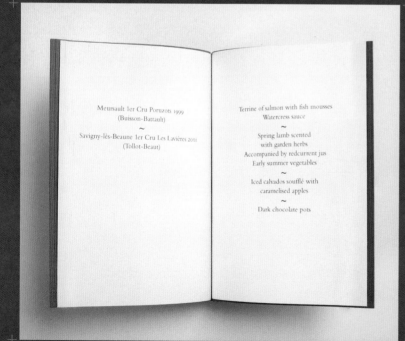

0571 ⇢ John & Orna Designs
    ⇢ UK

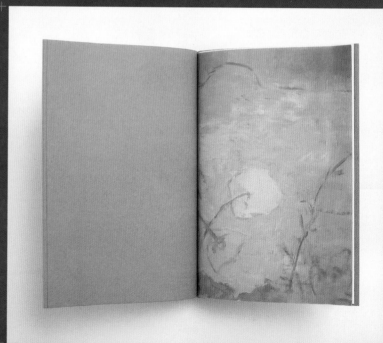

0572 ⇢ John & Orna Designs
    ⇢ UK

HAZEL AND DAVID ~ THE DECADES
Saturday 14 May 2005

LES TARTINES SALÉES
(servi avec marinade style grand-maman)

LaQuerbes
Rôti de bœuf froid, gruyère, compote d'oignons au balsamique, figue noire et sauce maison

LaBloomfield
Gravlax de saumon King bio, lard fumé, épinards et émulsion au galanga

LaChampagneur
Jambon de Parme, aubergines chinoises marinées, ricotta et sauce miso

LaWiseman
Thon Saku cru, avocat haché au couteau, yuzu, verdure et mayonaise au piment d'Espelette

LaStuart
Volaille de grain grillée, yogourt aux tomates confites à la sarriette et au fromage Manchego

LES TARTINES SUCRÉES

LaPommeCaramel
Compote de pommes Empire et cannelle en bâton, beurre fermier, caramel au Jack Daniel's

LaFraiseSzechuan
Purée de fraises au poivre de szechuan, fromage blanc à la lime et sucre en pain râpé

LaMarmelade
Marmelade d'agrumes mi-sucrée, crème fleurette à la truffe blanche

LA DENT SUCRÉE

LeFinancier
Financier tiède aux amandes de clémentines entières en purée et crème cuite à la cassonade

LaCrème
Crème brûlée classique à la vanille

LePannaCotta
Panna cotta au café, yogourt biologique nature et sablé à la cardamome

LeBiscuit
Biscuit davoine, ganache au chocolat noir de cacao (75%) et confiture de lait

SOUPES

LePanais
Crème de panais, huile de cari de Madras, brunoise de pomme fruit Golden et sel de céleri

LaLentille
Soupe de lentilles verte du Puy, pommes de terre ratte, légumes verts du moment et crème sûre au paprika fumé

LaPoule
Bouillon de poule bien réduit, orge biologique, pancetta rôtie et beaucoup de persil simple

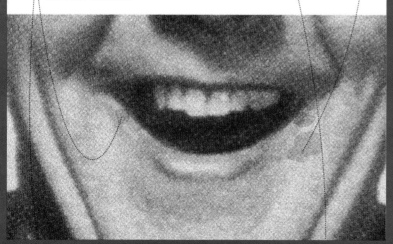

SALADES

Lépinard
Épinard bébé, antipasti, pamplemousse Ruby, menthe en feuille, vinaigrette minute au yogourt nature et miel de pommier

LaBette
Betteraves cuites entières, cresson, noix de pin rôties, huile de pistache première pression et vin cotto italien

LaRémoul
Rémoulade de légumes d'hiver, émulsion classique au citron, caperon et œuf de caille mariné au vieux xérès

LaFenouil
Copeaux de fenouil, tomates confites au sucre brut, macédoine de poire japonaise, huile de piment oiseau et pralin au sésame

LaBourbon
Mélange de laitue selon la saison, vinaigrette au cidre de glace et marinade d'oignons à la vanille Bourbon

PLATEAUX DE FROMAGE SELON L'ARRIVAGE ET GARNITURE STYLE TARTINE

(Purée de raisins rouges, noisettes rôties et croûtons de pain au noix)

LES GRILLES-FROMAGE

(choix de pains: grains germés bio, intégral bio, kamut bio ou classique bio)

LeVanHorne
Ketchup maison aux tomates épicées (vanille, cannelle, cumin, poivre), Victor et Berthold, amandes rôties d'Espagne et jeune pousse

LeLajoie
Purée de dattes de Mejold, compoté au poivre long, bacon fumé, vieux cheddar de l'Isle-aux-Grues

LeBernard
Chorizo XXX grillé, oignon sucré caramélisé, moutarde à la bière, chèvre noir vieilli

LeSt-Viateur
Légumes grillés au thym frais et marinés à l'huile d'olive au citron, fromage en grains

LeFairmount
Tomates séchées marinées, confit de canard au laurier, chèvre frais non-affiné et huile d'ail confit

LeLaurier
Salami à cru, fromage Pied-de-vent, purée d'herbe à la fleur de sel, abricot hydraté

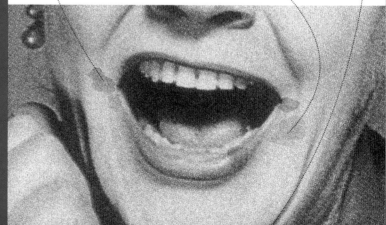

0576 --> Heather Heflin
--> USA

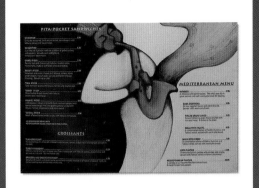

0577 --> Heather Heflin
--> USA

0578 --> Kapp & Associates, Inc.
--> USA

0579 --> Val Gene Associates
--> USA

0580 --> Val Gene Associates
--> USA

0581 --> Val Gene Associates
--> USA

0582 --> David Carter Design
--> USA

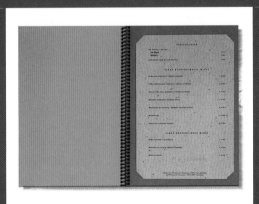

0583 --> David Carter Design
--> USA

0584 --> Sagmeister Inc.
--> USA

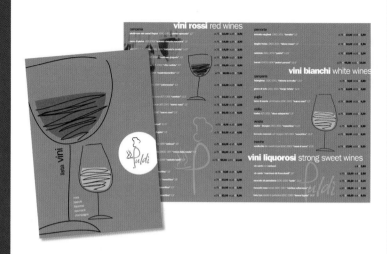

0585 →› bonbon london
    →› UK

0586 →› R&Mag Graphic Design
    →› Italy

0587 →› Hardy Design
    →› Brazil

0588 →› R&Mag Graphic Design
    →› Italy

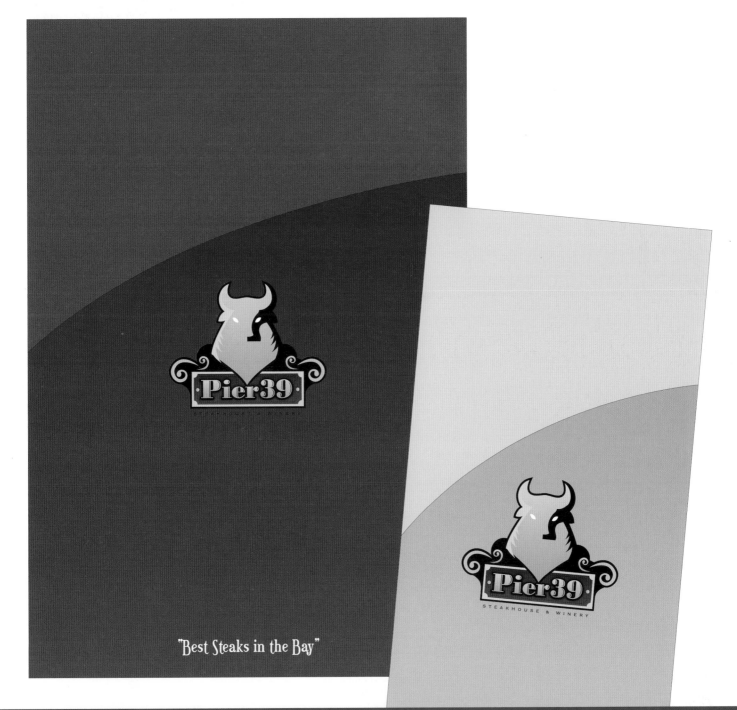

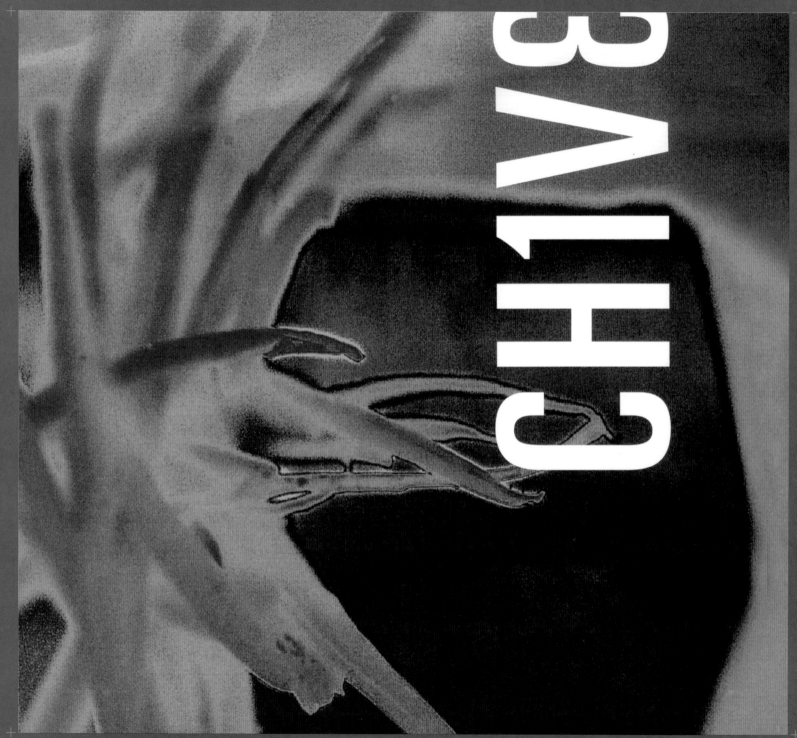

0590 ⇢ Hollis Brand Communications
⇢ USA

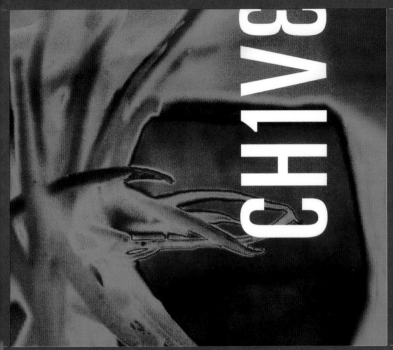

0591 --> Hollis Brand Communications
--> USA

0592 --> Mixer
--> Switzerland

0593 --> Warm Rain Ltd
--> UK

0594 --> Warm Rain Ltd
--> UK

0595 ···▷ The Levy Restaurants
···▷ USA

0596 ···▷ Disney Design Group
···▷ USA

0597 ···▷ Val Gene Associates
···▷ USA

0598 ···▷ Jeff Fisher LogoMotives
···▷ USA

0599 ···▷ Associates Design
···▷ USA

0600 ···▷ Ultra Design
···▷ USA

0601 ···▷ Smart Works
···▷ Australia

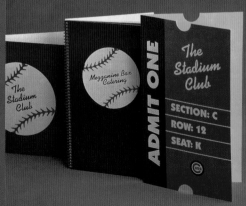

0602 ···▷ The Levy Restaurants
···▷ USA

0603 ···▷ Adrienne Weiss Corporation
···▷ USA

0604 ⇢ Let Her Press
⇢ USA

0605 ⇢ On The Edge Design, Inc
⇢ USA

THE OFFICIAL
MENU
FOR FAMISHED FANS

PIZZA
A 10-inch pizza, baked fresh and hot with your choice
of ham, beef or pepperoni topping. All include onions,
mushrooms, bell pepper and jalapeno peppers.
$8.20

BURGERS
Six ounces of fresh ground beef, charbroiled and
served dressed on a toasted bun. Served with fries.
$5.95   **with cheese $6.60**

POBOYS
Your choice of ham, roast beef or turkey on freshly-
baked French bread with lettuce, tomato, red onion
and pickles. Your choice of chips or fries.
$5.95

HOT DOG
A large, all-beef hot dog on Louisiana French bread
covered with chili, cheese and onions. Served with fries.
$4.95

CHIPOTLE CHICKEN TENDERS
A half-pound of tender chicken, fried to perfection
and served with blue cheese or ranch dipping sauce.
Served with fries.
$5.95

NACHOS
Crisp chips covered with chili, cheese and jalapenos.
$3.45

WINGS
Wings, grilled or fried, served either mild or hot,
with ranch dressing and celery sticks.
10 wings $6.95   20 wings $9.95

CHEESE FRIES
Heaps of freshly-cooked fries served
with melted cheddar cheese and jalapenos.
$2.95

CHIPS & SALSA
A pile of Mojo's crispy chips served with homemade

THE OFFICIAL
MENU
FOR FAMISHED FANS

PIZZA
A 10-inch pizza, baked fresh and hot with your choice
of ham, beef or pepperoni topping. All include onions,
mushrooms, bell pepper and jalapeno peppers.
$8.20

BURGERS
Six ounces of fresh ground beef, charbroiled and
served dressed on a toasted bun. Served with fries.
$5.95   **with cheese $6.60**

POBOYS
Your choice of ham, roast beef or turkey on freshly-
baked French bread with lettuce, tomato, red onion
and pickles. Your choice of chips or fries.
$5.95

HOT DOG
A large, all-beef hot dog on Louisiana French bread
covered with chili, cheese and onions. Served with fries.
$4.95

CHIPOTLE CHICKEN TENDERS
A half-pound of tender chicken, fried to perfection
and served with blue cheese or ranch dipping sauce.
Served with fries.
$5.95

NACHOS
Crisp chips covered with chili, cheese and jalapenos.
$3.45

WINGS
Wings, grilled or fried, served either mild or hot,
with ranch dressing and celery sticks.
10 wings $6.95   20 wings $9.95

CHEESE FRIES
Heaps of freshly-cooked fries served
with melted cheddar cheese and jalapenos.
$2.95

CHIPS & SALSA
A pile of Mojo's crispy chips served with homemade

THE OFFICIAL
MENU
FOR FAMISHED FANS

PIZZA
A 10-inch pizza, baked fresh and hot with your choice of ham, beef or pepperoni topping. All include onions, mushrooms, bell pepper and jalapeno peppers.
$8.20

BURGERS
Six ounces of fresh ground beef, charbroiled and served dressed on a toasted bun. Served with fries.
$5.95   **with cheese $6.60**

POBOYS
Your choice of ham, roast beef or turkey on freshly-baked French bread with lettuce, tomato, red onion and pickles. Your choice of chips or fries.
$5.95

HOT DOG
A large, all-beef hot dog on Louisiana French bread covered with chili, cheese and onions. Served with fries.
$4.95

CHIPOTLE CHICKEN TENDERS
A half-pound of tender chicken, fried to perfection and served with blue cheese or ranch dipping sauce. Served with fries.
$5.95

NACHOS
Crisp chips covered with chili, cheese and jalapenos.
$3.45

WINGS
Wings, grilled or fried, served either mild or hot, with ranch dressing and celery sticks.
10 wings $6.95   20 wings $9.95

CHEESE FRIES
Heaps of freshly-cooked fries served with melted cheddar cheese and jalapenos.
$2.95

CHIPS & SALSA

THE OFFICIAL
MENU
FOR FAMISHED FANS

PIZZA
A 10-inch pizza, baked fresh and hot with your choice of ham, beef or pepperoni topping. All include onions, mushrooms, bell pepper and jalapeno peppers.
$8.20

BURGERS
Six ounces of fresh ground beef, charbroiled and served dressed on a toasted bun. Served with fries.
$5.95   **with cheese $6.60**

POBOYS
Your choice of ham, roast beef or turkey on freshly-baked French bread with lettuce, tomato, red onion and pickles. Your choice of chips or fries.
$5.95

HOT DOG
A large, all-beef hot dog on Louisiana French bread covered with chili, cheese and onions. Served with fries.
$4.95

CHIPOTLE CHICKEN TENDERS
A half-pound of tender chicken, fried to perfection and served with blue cheese or ranch dipping sauce. Served with fries.
$5.95

NACHOS
Crisp chips covered with chili, cheese and jalapenos.
$3.45

WINGS
Wings, grilled or fried, served either mild or hot, with ranch dressing and celery sticks.
10 wings $6.95   20 wings $9.95

CHEESE FRIES
Heaps of freshly-cooked fries served with melted cheddar cheese and jalapenos.
$2.95

CHIPS & SALSA

0609 → Prejean Creative
→ USA

0610 ⇢ **Ultra Design**
⇢ USA

0611 ⇢ **Disney Design Group**
⇢ USA

0612 ⇢ **John Evans Design**
⇢ USA

0613 ⇢ **Disney Design Group**
⇢ USA

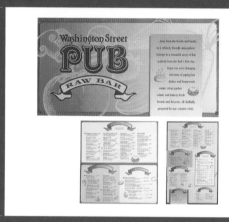

0614 ⇢ **Whitney-Edwards Design**
⇢ USA

0615 ⇢ **Disney Design Group**
⇢ USA

0616 ⇢ **PPA Design Limited**
⇢ Hong Kong

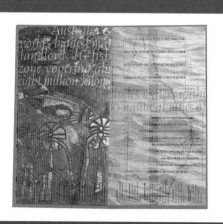

0617 ⇢ **PPA Design Limited**
⇢ Hong Kong

0618 ⇢ **Dean Johnson Design**
⇢ USA

0621 ⋯→ Associates Design
⋯→ USA

0622 ⋯→ Associates Design
⋯→ USA

0623 ⋯→ Associates Design
⋯→ USA

0624 ⋯→ Pentagram Design
⋯→ USA

0625 ⋯→ Pentagram Design
⋯→ USA

0626 ⋯→ Annabelle Wimer Design
⋯→ USA

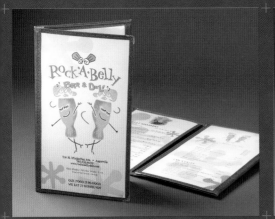

0627 ⋯→ S&N Design
⋯→ USA

0628 ⋯→ S&N Design
⋯→ USA

0629 ⋯→ Fabrice Praeger
⋯→ France

0631 ⇢ Sayles Graphic Design
⇢ USA

0632 ⇢ The Levy Restaurants
⇢ USA

0633 ⇢ Raidy Printing Company SAL
⇢ Lebanon

0634 ⇢ Schumaker
⇢ USA

0635 ⇢ The Levy Restaurants
⇢ USA

0636 ⇢ Corbin Design
⇢ USA

0637 ⇢ PM Design
⇢ USA

0638 ⇢ PPA Design Limited
⇢ Hong Kong

0639 ⇢ Richard Poulin Design Group
⇢ USA

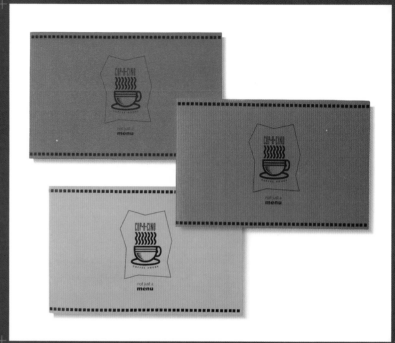

0640 ⟶ PPA Design Limited
    ⟶ Hong Kong

0641 ⟶ Gloria Paul
    ⟶ USA

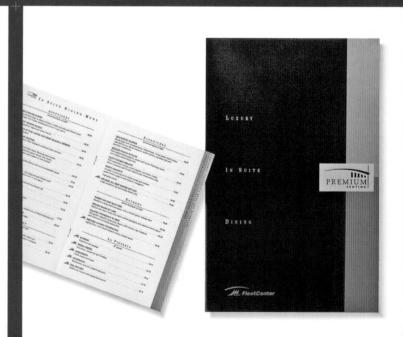

0642 ⟶ Associates Advertising
    ⟶ USA

0643 ⟶ Associates Design
    ⟶ USA

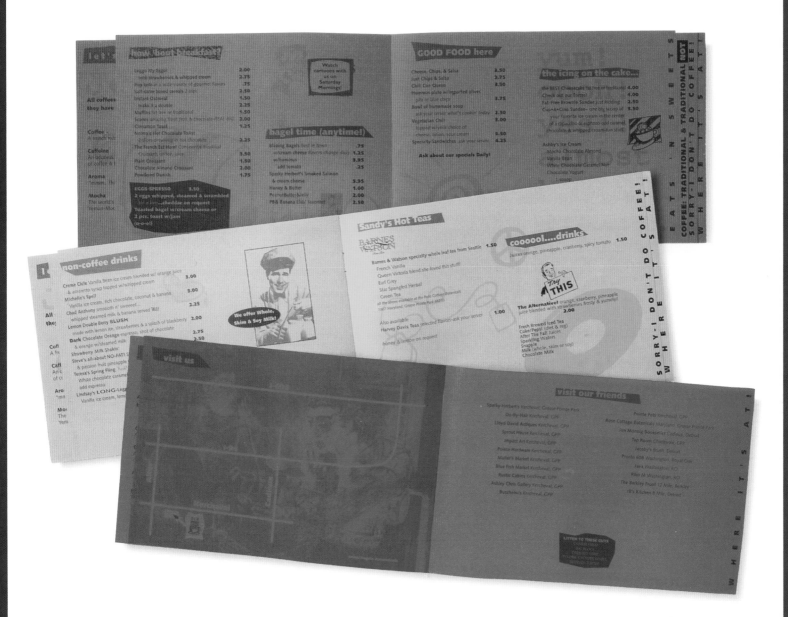

0645 ⋯➔ Richard Poulin Design Group
⋯➔ USA

0646 ⋯➔ XJR Design
⋯➔ USA

0647 ⋯➔ David Carter Design
⋯➔ USA

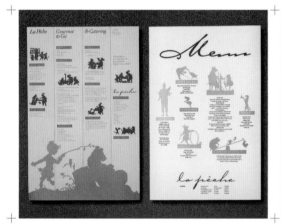

0648 ⋯➔ Bullet Communications Inc
⋯➔ USA

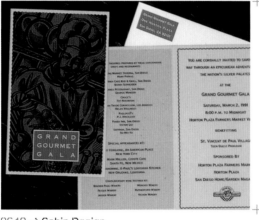

0649 ⋯➔ Sabin Design
⋯➔ USA

0650 ⋯➔ The Levy Restaurants
⋯➔ USA

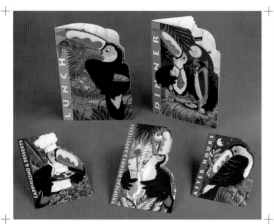

0651 ⋯➔ Adventure Advertising
⋯➔ USA

0652 ⋯➔ Sayles Graphic Design
⋯➔ USA

0653 ⋯➔ On The Edge Design, Inc
⋯➔ USA

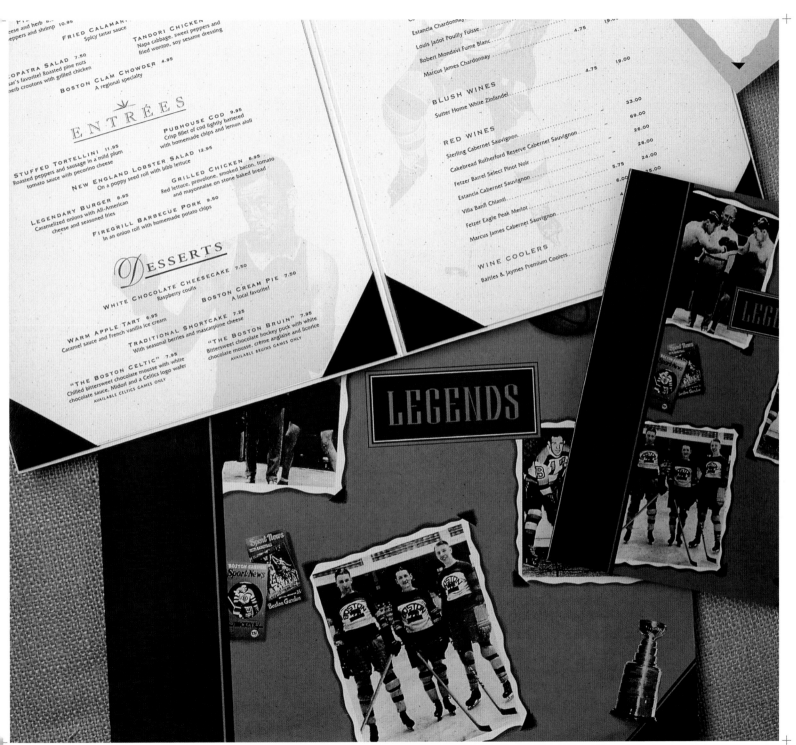

PI...
...eese and herb 8...
...eppers and shrimp 10.95

FRIED CALAMAR...
Spicy tartar sauce

TANDORI CHICKEN...
Napa cabbage, sweet peppers and
fried wonton, soy sesame dressing

...OPATRA SALAD 7.50
...sar's favorite! Roasted pine nuts
...herb croutons with grilled chicken

BOSTON CLAM CHOWDER 4.95
A regional specialty

ENTRÉES

STUFFED TORTELLINI 11.95
Roasted peppers and sausage in a mild plum
tomato sauce with pecorino cheese

PUBHOUSE COD 9.95
Crisp fillet of cod lightly battered
with homemade chips and lemon aioli

NEW ENGLAND LOBSTER SALAD 12.95
On a poppy seed roll with bibb lettuce

GRILLED CHICKEN 8.95
Red lettuce, provolone, smoked bacon, tomato
and mayonnaise on stone baked bread

LEGENDARY BURGER 8.95
Caramelized onions with All-American
cheese and seasoned fries

FIREGRILL BARBECUE PORK 9.50
In an onion roll with homemade potato chips

DESSERTS

WHITE CHOCOLATE CHEESECAKE 7.50
Raspberry coulis

BOSTON CREAM PIE 7.50
A local favorite!

WARM APPLE TART 6.95
Caramel sauce and French vanilla ice cream

TRADITIONAL SHORTCAKE 7.25
With seasonal berries and mascarpone cheese

"THE BOSTON BRUIN" 7.95
Bittersweet chocolate hockey puck with white
chocolate mousse, creme anglaise and licorice
AVAILABLE BRUINS GAMES ONLY

"THE BOSTON CELTIC" 7.95
Chilled bittersweet chocolate mousse with white
chocolate sauce, Midori and a Celtics logo wafer
AVAILABLE CELTICS GAMES ONLY

Estancia Chardonnay .... 19.0...
Louis Jadot Pouilly Fuisse 4.75
Robert Mondavi Fume Blanc
Marcus James Chardonnay 4.75   19.00

BLUSH WINES
Sutter Home White Zinfandel 33.00

RED WINES
                                                        69.00
Sterling Cabernet Sauvignon 26.00
Cakebread Rutherford Reserve Cabernet Sauvignon ... 26.00
Fetzer Barrel Select Pinot Noir 24.00
Estancia Cabernet Sauvignon .... 5.75 ...25.00
Villa Banfi Chianti 6.00
Fetzer Eagle Peak Merlot
Marcus James Cabernet Sauvignon

WINE COOLERS
Bartles & Jaymes Premium Coolers ....

LEGENDS

0655 ⇢ Associates Design
⇢ USA

0656 ⇢ Mind's Eye Studio
⇢ Canada

0657 ⇢ Eilts Anderson Tracy
⇢ USA

0658 ⇢ Mind's Eye Studio
⇢ Canada

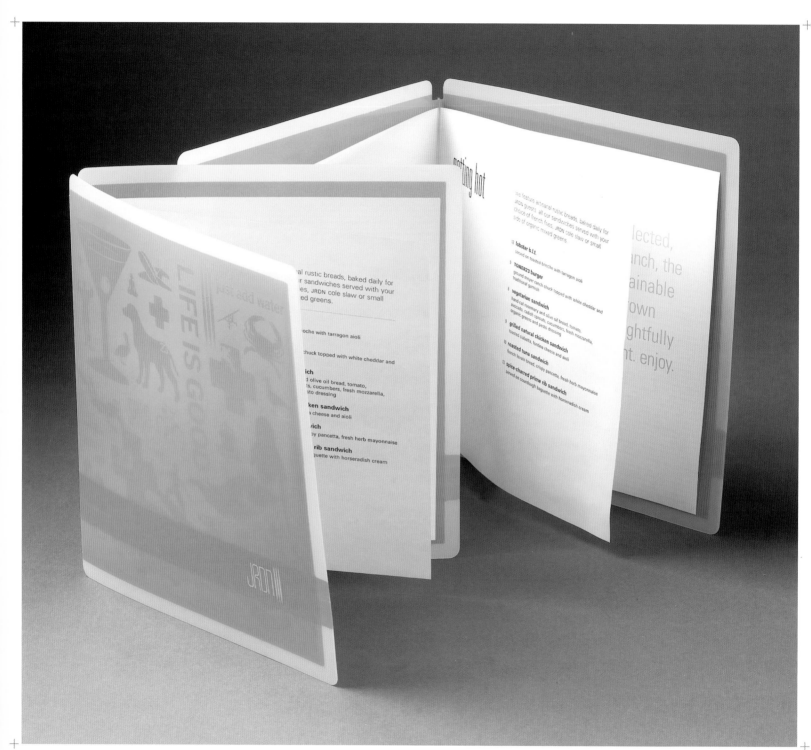

0661 ···> McCord Graphic Design
···> Country unavailable

0662 ···> Bright & Associates
···> USA

0663 ···> Associates Design
···> USA

0664 ···> Associates Design
···> USA

0665 ···> Shamlian Advertising
···> USA

0666 ···> Marve Cooper Design, Ltd.
···> USA

0667 ···> Emma Main
···> New Zealand

0668 ···> PPA Design Ltd
···> Hong Kong

0669 ···> PPA Design Ltd
···> Hong Kong

04

0670–0728 →

CHAPTER 4
PACKAGING

BAGS
BOXES
CARTONS
BOTTLES
WRAPPERS

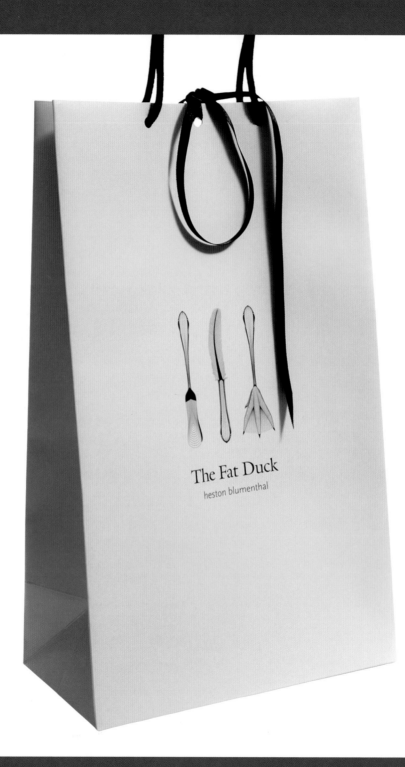

0671 ⇢ Inaria
   ⇢ UK

0672 ⇢ Hornall Anderson Design Works
   ⇢ USA

0673 ⇢ LM
   ⇢ UK

0674 ⇢ CDI Studios
   ⇢ USA

0675 ⋯⇥ David Caunce
⋯⇥ UK

0676 ⋯⇥ David Caunce
⋯⇥ UK

0677 ⋯⇥ David Caunce
⋯⇥ UK

0678 ⋯⇥ Warm Rain Ltd
⋯⇥ UK

0681 ⋯→ Artie Horowitz Design
⋯→ USA

0682 ⋯→ bonbon london
⋯→ UK

0683 ⋯→ Bullet Communications Inc.
⋯→ USA

0684 ⋯→ Public
⋯→ USA

0685 ⋯→ biz-R
⋯→ UK

0686 ⋯→ R&Mag Graphic Design
⋯→ Italy

0687 ⋯→ bonbon london
⋯→ UK

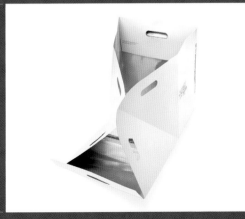

0688 ⋯→ bonbon london
⋯→ UK

0689 ⋯→ bonbon london
⋯→ UK

0690 ⋯⋯→ Inaria
⋯⋯→ UK

0691 ⋯⋯→ Warm Rain Ltd
⋯⋯→ UK

0692 ⋯⋯→ Warm Rain Ltd
⋯⋯→ UK

0693 ⋯⋯→ Warm Rain Ltd
⋯⋯→ UK

0696 ⋯⋯> BigEyes Design
⋯⋯> Israel

0697 ⋯⋯> BigEyes Design
⋯⋯> Israel

0698 ⋯⋯> sky design
⋯⋯> USA

0699 ⋯⋯> sky design
⋯⋯> USA

0700 ···∌ BigEyes Design
···∌ Israel

0701 ···∌ David Caunce
···∌ UK

0702 ···∌ David Caunce
···∌ UK

0703 ···∌ Rome & Gold Creative
···∌ USA

0704 ···∌ Rome & Gold Creative
···∌ USA

0705 ···∌ Rome & Gold Creative
···∌ USA

0706 ···∌ Willoughby Design Group
···∌ USA

0707 ···∌ Hornall Anderson Design Works
···∌ USA

0708 ···∌ Hornall Anderson Design Works
···∌ USA

0711 ⇢ Hornall Anderson Design Works
⇢ USA

0712 ⇢ Hornall Anderson Design Works
⇢ USA

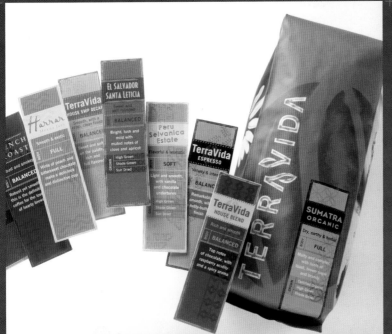

0713 ⇢ Hornall Anderson Design Works
⇢ USA

0714 ⇢ Evenson Design Group
⇢ USA

0716 ⇢ Vrontikis Design Office
    ⇢ USA

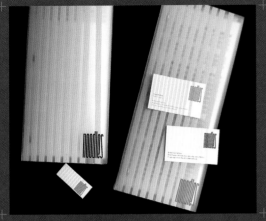

0720 ···> Mimolimit
···> Czech Republic

0721 ···> Hans Flink Design Inc.
···> USA

0722 ···> Hans Flink Design Inc.
···> USA

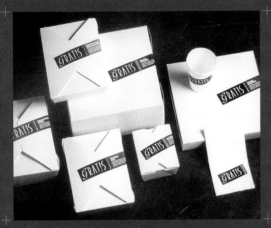

0723 ···> Bright & Associates
···> USA

0724 ···> Regan Blough
···> USA

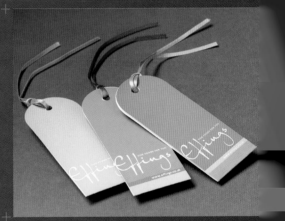

0725 ···> biz-R
···> UK

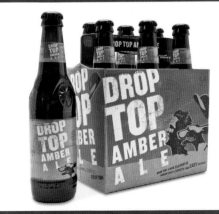

0726 ···> Hornall Anderson Design Works
···> USA

0727 ···> Hornall Anderson Design Works
···> USA

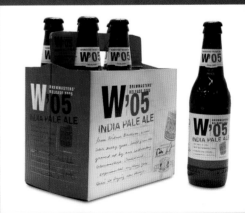

0728 ···> Hornall Anderson Design Works
···> USA

05

07729-08996 →→

CHAPTER 5
PROMOTIONAL ITEMS

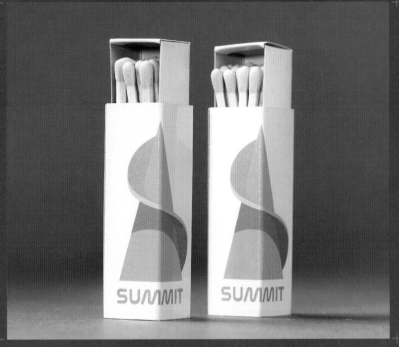

0730 ⇢ Mirko Ilić Corp.
    ⇢ USA

0731 ⇢ Graphic Content
    ⇢ USA

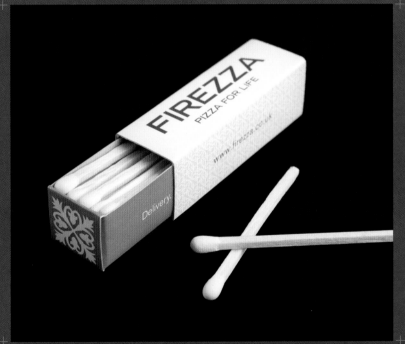

0732 ⇢ Inaria
    ⇢ UK

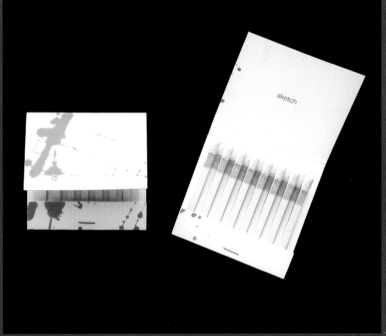

0733 ⇢ Warm Rain Ltd
    ⇢ UK

0734 ⋯⇥ bonbon london
⋯⇥ UK

0735 ⋯⇥ 804© Graphic Design
⋯⇥ Germany

0736 ⋯⇥ Regan Blough
⋯⇥ USA

0737 ⋯⇥ Mirko Ilić Corp.
⋯⇥ USA

0739 ⋯⟩ i_d buero
⋯⟩ Germany

0740 ⟶ Turnstyle
⋯⟩ USA

0741 ⋯⟩ CWA Inc.
⋯⟩ USA

0742 ⋯⟩ Northern Artisan
⋯⟩ USA

0743 ⋯⟩ Ducks Design
⋯⟩ Germany

0744 ⋯⟩ Louise Fili Ltd.
⋯⟩ USA

0745 ⋯⟩ Raidy Printing Group SAL
⋯⟩ Lebanon

0746 ⟶ Pentagram
⋯⟩ USA

0747 ⋯⟩ Vrontikis Design Office
⋯⟩ USA

0749 ⇢ AdamsMorioka
   ⇢ USA

0750 ⇢ AdamsMorioka
   ⇢ USA

0751 ⇢ Finest/Magma
   ⇢ Germany

0752 ⇢ Finest/Magma
   ⇢ Germany

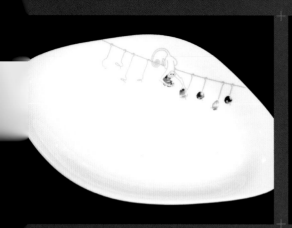

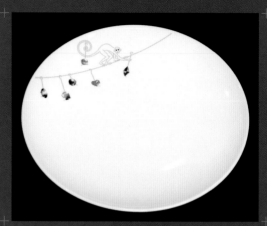

0754 →• Mirko Ilić Corp.
⋯→ USA

0755 →• Mirko Ilić Corp.
⋯→ USA

0756 →• Mirko Ilić Corp.
⋯→ USA

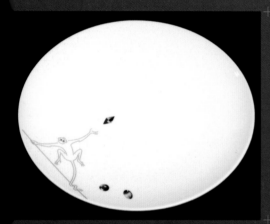

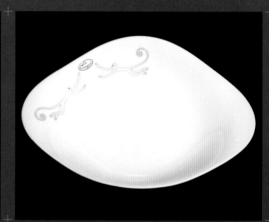

0757 →• Mirko Ilić Corp.
⋯→ USA

0758 →• Mirko Ilić Corp.
⋯→ USA

0759 →• Mirko Ilić Corp.
⋯→ USA

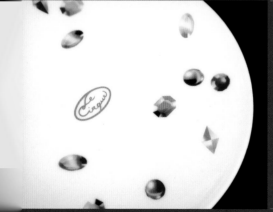

0760 →• Mirko Ilić Corp.
⋯→ USA

0761 →• Mirko Ilić Corp.
⋯→ USA

0762 →• Mirko Ilić Corp.
⋯→ USA

0763 ⇢ Mirko Ilić Corp.
⇢ USA

MARCI BREITLING & BOB FINLAYSON
INVITE YOU TO CELEBRATE
THE V.I.P. GRAND OPENING OF

TASTINGS
A new concept in fine food and wine

THURSDAY, OCTOBER 20, 2005
6:30 IN THE EVENING

ATRIUM AT 69930 HIGHWAY 111
NCHO MIRAGE, CALIFORNIA

SE R.S.V.P. JANET NEWCOMB
200.8684 BY OCTOBER 15

COCKTAIL ATTIRE

TASTINGS

0765 ···→ **Mirko Ilić Corp.**
   ···→ USA

0766 ···→ **Mimolimit**
   ···→ Czech Republic

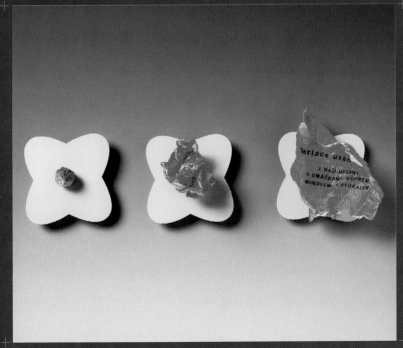

0767 ···→ **Mimolimit**
   ···→ Czech Republic

0768 ···→ **Rome & Gold Creative**
   ···→ USA

0770 ⟶ 804© Graphic Design
⟶ Germany

0771 ⟶ Nita B. Creative
⟶ USA

0774 ⋯⋙ bonbon london
⋯⋙ UK

0775 ⋯⋙ On The Edge Design, Inc
⋯⋙ USA

0776 ⋯⋙ Ultra Design
⋯⋙ USA

0777 ⋯⋙ Hollis Brand Communications
⋯⋙ USA

0780 ··▷ Public
··▷ USA

0781 ··▷ Dornig Graphic Design
··▷ Austria

0782 ··▷ Warm Rain Ltd
··▷ UK

0783 ··▷ On The Edge Design, Inc
··▷ USA

0784 ··▷ Hollis Brand Communications
··▷ USA

0785 ··▷ biz-R
··▷ UK

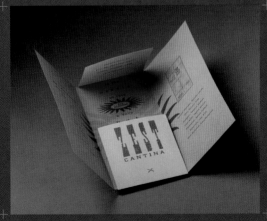

0786 ··▷ Braue Strategic Brand Design
··▷ Germany

0787 ··▷ Vrontikis Design Office
··▷ USA

0788 ··▷ On The Edge Design, Inc
··▷ USA

CAF53AR

**CAF53AR FÜNFDREI
AMALIENSTRASSE 53   76133 KARLSRUHE
WWW.FUENFDREI.DE**

0789 ⇢ Finest/Magma
⇢ Germany

TREU530NUS

ab zehn mal fünfdrei
gibt es ein getränk bis 5,30 € umsonst!

0790 ⇢ Finest/Magma
⇢ Germany

AFTERWORK.START
MITTWOCHS
18-21 UHR
CAFEBAR FÜNFDREI

53

SNACKS GRATIS
UND FREIER EINTRITT IM E-CLUB

AB 19.10.2005

0791 ⇢ Finest/Magma
⇢ Germany

0792 ⇢ Hollis Brand Communications
⇢ USA

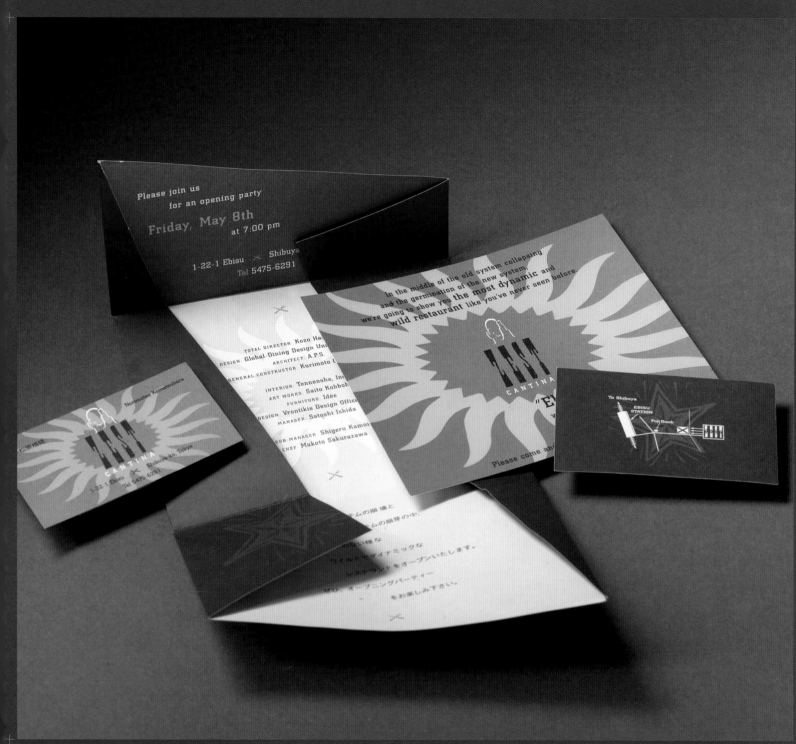

0795 ⇢ bonbon london
⇢ UK

0796 ⇢ bonbon london
⇢ UK

0797 ⇢ On The Edge Design, Inc
⇢ USA

0798 ⇢ On The Edge Design, Inc
⇢ USA

0799 →❖ Rome & Gold Creative
→❖ USA

0800 →❖ Warm Rain Ltd
→❖ UK

0801 →❖ Crush Design & Art Direction
→❖ UK

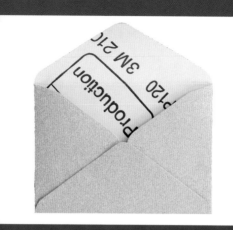

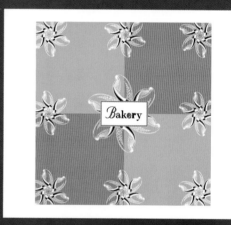

0802 →❖ BigEyes Design
→❖ Israel

0803 →❖ Hollis Brand Communications
→❖ USA

0804 →❖ BigEyes Design
→❖ Israel

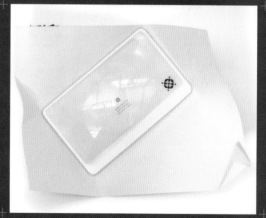

0805 →❖ Ducks Design
→❖ Germany

0806 →❖ Brandhouse WTS
→❖ UK

0807 →❖ Brandhouse WTS
→❖ UK

0809 ⋯➔ Hollis Brand Communications
⋯➔ USA

0810 ···› Brandhouse WTS
    ···› UK

0811 ···› R&Mag Graphic Design
    ···› Italy

0812 ···› Frost Design, Sydney
    ···› Australia

0813 ···› Fresh Oil
    ···› USA

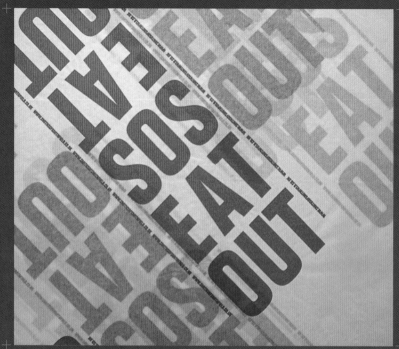

0814 ⋯➔ bonbon london
   ⋯➔ UK

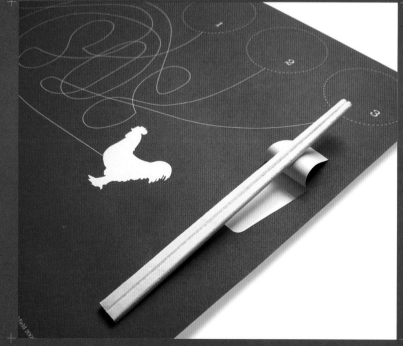

0815 ⋯➔ bonbon london
   ⋯➔ UK

0816 ⋯➔ bonbon london
   ⋯➔ UK

0819 --> Crush Design & Art Direction
--> UK

0820 --> Turnstyle
--> USA

0821 --> Vrontikis Design Office
--> USA

0822 --> Willoughby Design Group
--> USA

0823 --> Willoughby Design Group
--> USA

0824 --> David Caunce
--> UK

0825 --> Hand Made Group
--> Italy

0826 --> R&Mag Graphic Design
--> Italy

0827 --> Fresh Oil
--> USA

sangre

saturdays @ kanela

Kanela

0832 ⋯→ Octavo Design Pty Ltd
⋯→ Australia

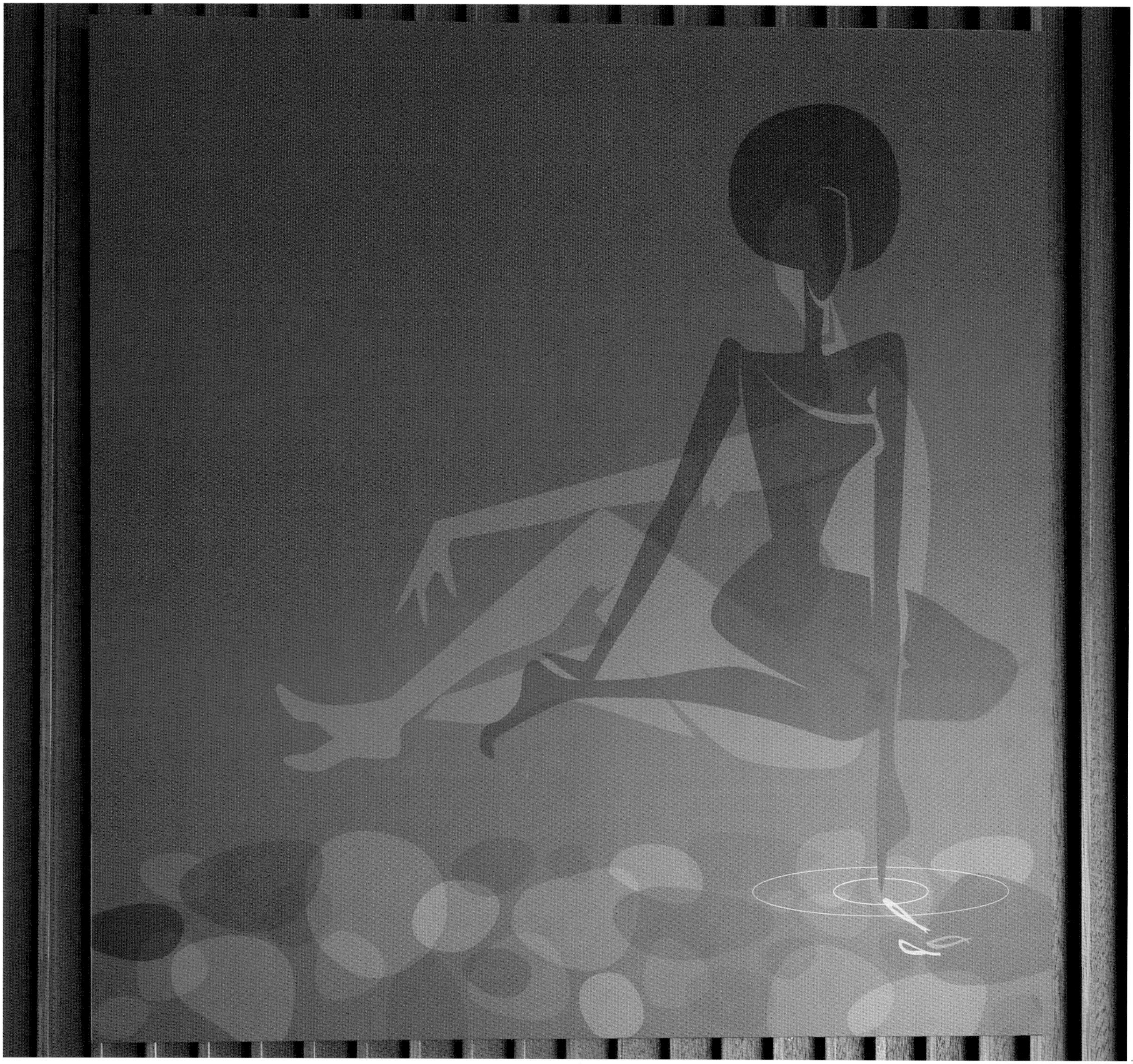

0833 ···> Smart Works
···> Australia

0834 ⇢ bonbon london
⇢ UK

0835 ⇢ Elfen
⇢ Wales

0836 ⇢ Hornall Anderson Design Works
⇢ USA

0837 ⇢ Rome & Gold Creative
⇢ USA

0838 ⇢ Rome & Gold Creative
⇢ USA

0839 ⇢ Rome & Gold Creative
⇢ USA

0840 ···> **Rome & Gold Creative**
    ···> USA

0841 ···> **Rome & Gold Creative**
    ···> USA

0842 → Northern Artisan
→ USA

0843 → Bartosz Oczujda
→ Poland

0844 → Warm Rain Ltd
→ UK

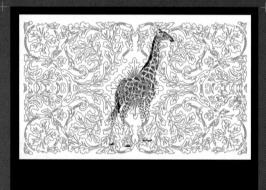

0845 → Warm Rain Ltd
→ UK

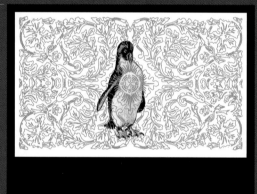

0846 → Warm Rain Ltd
→ UK

0847 → Warm Rain Ltd
→ UK

0848 → Warm Rain Ltd
→ UK

0849 → Warm Rain Ltd
→ UK

0850 → Warm Rain Ltd
→ UK

Von nun an schwingt der Sohn die Kelle!

Grafik: Erich Brechbühl (www.mixer.ch)

0853 ⇢ Hornall Anderson Design Works
⇢ USA

0854 ⇢ Hornall Anderson Design Works
⇢ USA

0855 ⇢ Hornall Anderson Design Works
⇢ USA

0856 ⇢ Hornall Anderson Design Works
⇢ USA

0857 ⋯➔ Threefold
⋯➔ Australia

0858 ⋯➔ Spark Studios Pty Ltd
⋯➔ Australia

0859 ⋯➔ BASELINE
⋯➔ Scotland

0860 ⋯➔ Laura Jacoby
⋯➔ USA

Vue de Monde

EDELBITTER KUVERTÜRE
ORANGE–PISTAZIEN

Theatercafe
BREGENZ·AUSTRIA

EDELBITTER KUVERTÜRE
GHANA 85

Theatercafe
BREGENZ·AUSTRIA

EDELBITTER KUVERTÜRE
CHILI

Theatercafe
BREGENZ·AUSTRIA

EDELMILCH
MAKADAMIA–NUSS

Theatercafe
BREGENZ·AUSTRIA

BIO-EDELMILCH
CASHEW–NUSS

Theatercafe
BREGENZ·AUSTRIA

EDELMILCH

Theatercafe
BREGENZ·AUSTRIA

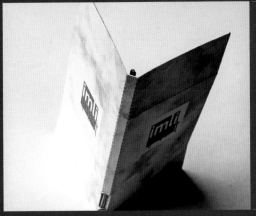

0863 ⇢ Warm Rain Ltd
⇢ UK

0864 ⇢ Warm Rain Ltd
⇢ UK

0865 ⇢ Smart Works
⇢ Australia

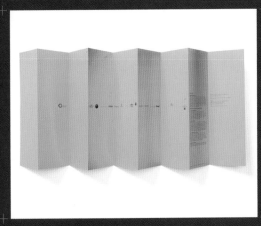

0866 ⇢ Frost Design, Sydney
⇢ Australia

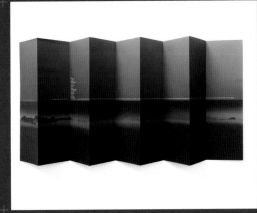

0867 ⇢ Frost Design, Sydney
⇢ Australia

0868 ⇢ Frost Design, Sydney
⇢ Australia

0869 ⇢ Vrontikis Design Office
⇢ USA

0870 ⇢ Ducks Design
⇢ Germany

0871 ⇢ bonbon london
⇢ UK

0873 ···➔ Rome & Gold Creative
    ···➔ USA

0874 ···➔ Rome & Gold Creative
    ···➔ USA

0875 ···➔ Evenson Design Group
    ···➔ USA

0876 ···➔ CDI Studios
    ···➔ USA

0878 ⇢ bonbon london
⇢ UK

0879 ⇢ On The Edge Design, Inc
⇢ USA

0880 ⇢ Lodge Design Company
⇢ USA

0881 ⇢ Campus Collection
⇢ USA

0882 ⇢ Fullblastinc.com
⇢ USA

0883 ⇢ Campus Collection
⇢ USA

0884 ⇢ On The Edge Design, Inc
⇢ USA

0885 ⇢ Campus Collection
⇢ USA

0886 ⇢ On The Edge Design, Inc
⇢ USA

0888 ⋯→ **On The Edge Design, Inc**
⋯→ USA

0889 ⋯→ **Campus Collection**
⋯→ USA

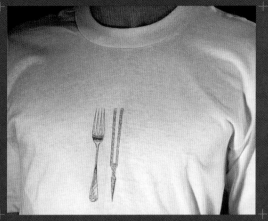

0890 ⋯→ **Sagmeister Inc**
⋯→ USA

0891 ⋯→ **Campus Collection**
⋯→ USA

0892 ⋯→ **On The Edge Design, Inc**
⋯→ USA

0893 ⋯→ **On The Edge Design, Inc**
⋯→ USA

06

0897-1.0000 ⇢
0897-0890 ⇢

CHAPTER 6
STATIONERY

BUSINESS CARDS
LETTERHEAD
FOLDERS
ENVELOPES

Sonny Ahuja
gourmand

8751 W. Charleston Blvd
Suite 110
Las Vegas, Nevada 89117

702+363+2538 Phone
702+248+2538 Facsimile
(BLEU)

Email sonny@bleugourmet.com
Wsite   www.bleugourmet.com

0898 ⟶ **i_d buero**
⟶ Germany

0899 ⟶ **i_d buero**
⟶ Germany

0900 ⟶ **Fabrice Praeger**
⟶ France

0901 ⟶ **804© Graphic Design**
⟶ Germany

0902 ⟶ **christiansen: creative**
⟶ USA

0903 ⟶ **Public**
⟶ USA

0904 ⟶ **Public**
⟶ USA

0905 ⟶ **bonbon london**
⟶ UK

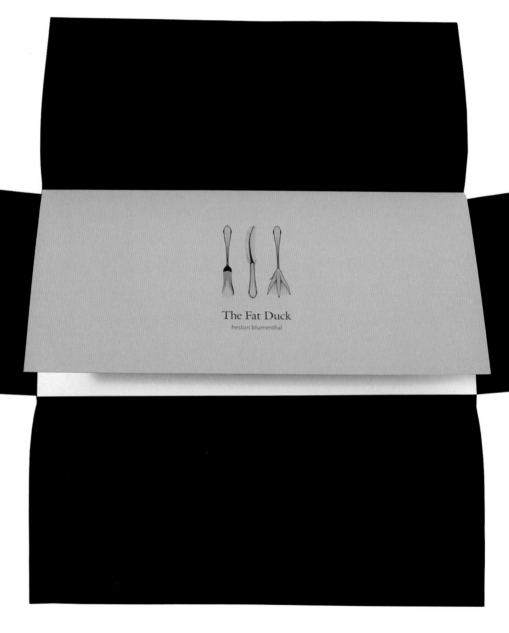

The Fat Duck
heston blumenthal

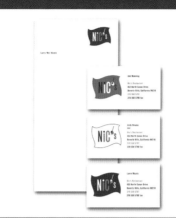

0908 ⇢ **i_d buero**
⇢ Germany

0909 ⇢ **The Design Laboratory**
⇢ UK

0910 ⇢ **AdamsMorioka**
⇢ USA

0911 ⇢ **Spark Studio Pty Ltd**
⇢ Australia

0912 ⇢ **DZ6 Design**
⇢ Brazil

0913 ⇢ **Fabrice Praeger**
⇢ France

0914 ⇢ **Bakken Creative Company**
⇢ USA

0915 ⇢ **Bakken Creative Company**
⇢ USA

0916 ⇢ **Smart Works**
⇢ Australia

SMELLING MISTAKE.

WINE MAKES YOU HAPPY.

Vue de Monde

VUE DE MONDE · NORMANBY CHAMBERS
430 LITTLE COLLINS ST MELBOURNE VIC 3000
TELEPHONE 03 9691 3888 FACSIMILE 03 9600 4600
vuedemonde@vuedemonde.com.au www.vuedemonde.com.au

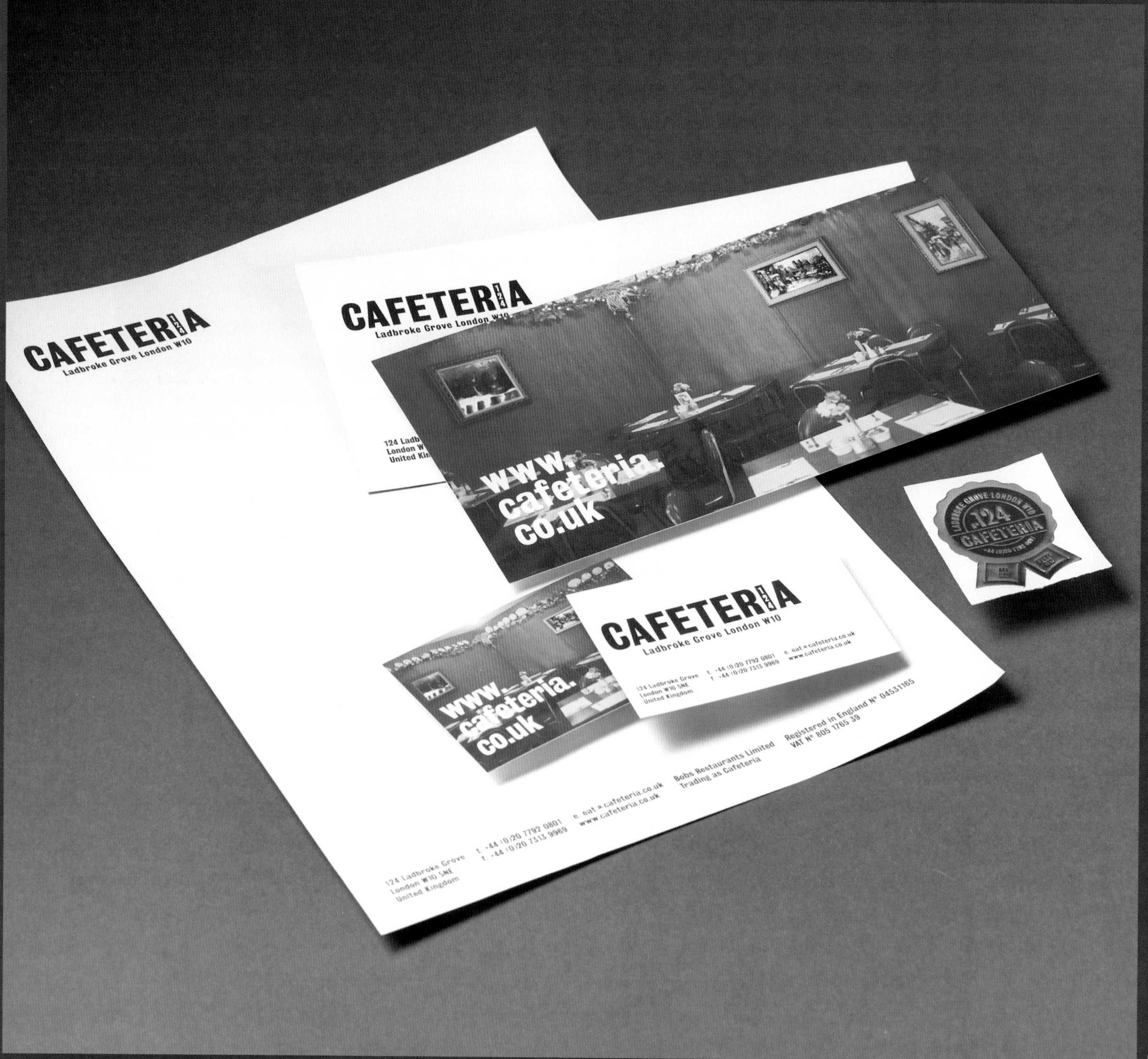

0922 → **bonbon london**
→ UK

0923 ···> **Hardy Design**
···> Brazil

0924 ···> **bonbon london**
···> UK

0925 ···> **bonbon london**
···> UK

0926 ···> **urban INFLUENCE design studio**
···> USA

0927 ···> **urban INFLUENCE design studio**
···> USA

0928 ···> **Warm Rain Ltd**
···> USA

0929 ···> **On The Edge Design, Inc**
···> USA

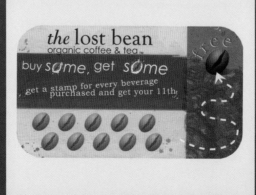

0930 ···> **On The Edge Design, Inc**
···> USA

0931 ···> **On The Edge Design, Inc**
···> USA

0932 ⇢ **Fabrice Praeger**
⇢ France

0933 ⇢ **Fabrice Praeger**
⇢ France

0934 ⇢ **Fabrice Praeger**
⇢ France

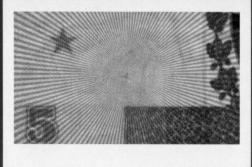

0935 ⇢ **Public**
⇢ USA

0936 ⇢ **Public**
⇢ USA

0937 ⇢ **Public**
⇢ USA

0938 ⇢ **Public**
⇢ USA

0939 ⇢ **Public**
⇢ USA

0940 ⇢ **Public**
⇢ USA

0941 ···> Bowhaus Design Groupe
··> USA

0942 ···> From Scratch Design Studio
··> USA

0943 ···> From Scratch Design Studio
··> USA

0944 ···> Hollis Brand Communications
··> USA

0945 ···> Hollis Brand Communications
··> USA

0946 ···> bonbon london
··> UK

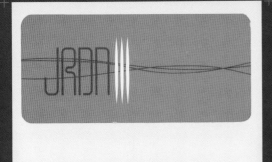

0947 ···> Hollis Brand Communications
··> USA

0948 ···> Hollis Brand Communications
··> USA

0949 ···> bonbon london
··> UK

0950 ⇢ **Fullblastinc.com**
⇢ USA

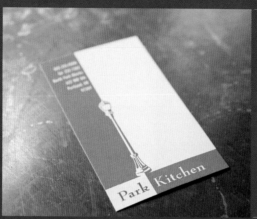

0951 ⇢ **Fullblastinc.com**
⇢ USA

0952 ⇢ **Braue Strategic Brand Design**
⇢ Germany

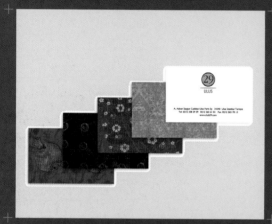

0953 ⇢ **Ayse Çelem**
⇢ Turkey

0954 ⇢ **S&N Design**
⇢ USA

0955 ⇢ **David Caunce**
⇢ UK

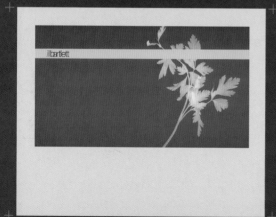

0956 ⇢ **bonbon london**
⇢ UK

0957 ⇢ **bonbon london**
⇢ UK

0958 ⇢ **bonbon london**
⇢ UK

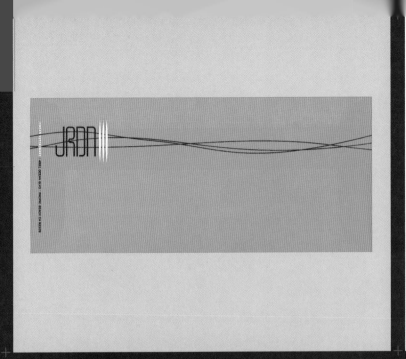

13011 Newport Ave. #104

Tustin, CA 92780

Ph: 714-544-2584

Fax: 714-544-2586

info@thelostbean.com

www.thelostbean.com

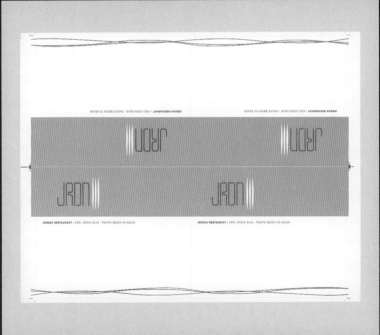

JORDAN RESTAURANT : 4951 OCEAN BLVD : PACIFIC BEACH CA 92109

JORDAN RESTAURANT : 4951 OCEAN BLVD : PACIFIC BEACH CA 92109

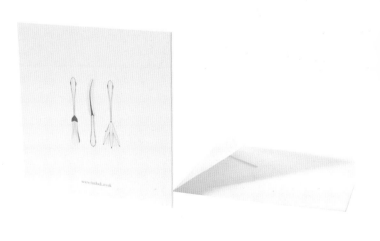

www.bonbd.co.uk

0963 ⇢ **Lodge Design Company**
⇢ USA

0964 ⇢ **i_d buero**
⇢ Germany

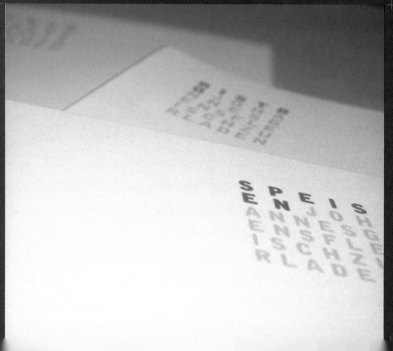

0969 ⤳ **Poulin & Morris**
⤳ USA

0970 ⤏ **Octavo Design Pty Ltd**
⤏ Australia

0971 ⤳ **Octavo Design Pty Ltd**
⤳ Australia

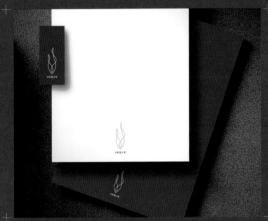

0972 ⤳ **Octavo Design Pty Ltd**
⤳ Australia

0973 ⤏ **Inaria**
⤏ UK

0974 ⤳ **Willoughby Design Group**
⤳ USA

0975 ⤳ **Willoughby Design Group**
⤳ USA

0976 ⤳ **Bakken Creative Company**
⤳ USA

0977 ⤳ **Hollis Brand Communications**
⤳ USA

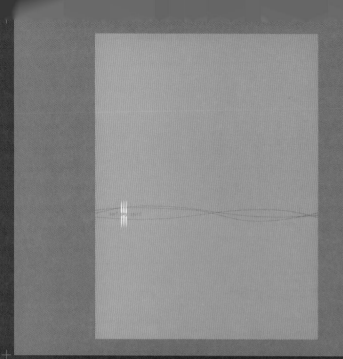

0978 ⇢ **Hollis Brand Communications**
⇢ USA

So This Friend of Mine Was Going To A Sunday Brunch And She Decided To Bring Along Her Great Aunt's Famous Coffee Cake. Only, It Wasn't Really Her Aunt's Secret Recipe. It Was More Like A Friend Of Her Aunt's, Who'd Passed It on To Her Aunt, Who Passed It On To My Friend. (We Like to Call That *Three Degrees*) Anyway, She gets To The Brunch And Sees Three OTHeR People Also Brought "Her" Aunt'S Famous Coffee Cake. NoT Surprising. Around Here Everybody Pretty Much KNows Everybody. And A Good Thing Gets Around.

0979 ⇢ **Bakken Creative Company**
⇢ USA

JRDN ‖‖

surf:sky:spirit

0980 ⇢ **Hollis Brand Communications**
⇢ USA

RESTAURANT | BAR | LOUNGE

REALTO
XXXI.MMIII

0981 ⇢ **Ducks Design**
⇢ Germany

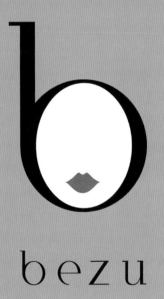

bezu

FRENCH-ASIAN CUISINE

0982 ⋯⋙ From Scratch Design Studio
⋯⋙ USA

0983 ⋯➔ The Design Laboratory
⋯➔ UK

0984 ⋯➔ The Design Laboratory
⋯➔ UK

0985 ⋯➔ Warm Rain Ltd
⋯➔ UK

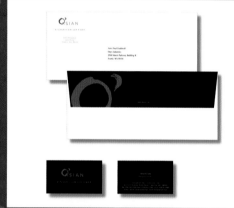

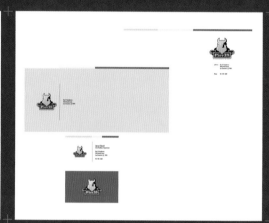

0986 ⋯➔ Crush Design & Art Direction
⋯➔ UK

0987 ⋯➔ Mary Hutchinson Design LLC
⋯➔ USA

0988 ⋯➔ Graphicwise Inc
⋯➔ USA

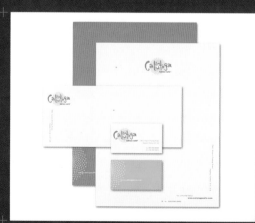

0989 ⋯➔ AdamsMorioka
⋯➔ USA

0990 ⋯➔ Hardy Design
⋯➔ Brazil

0991 ⋯➔ Vrontikis Design Office
⋯➔ USA

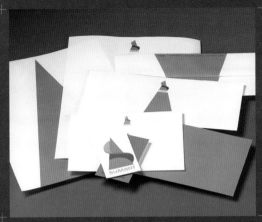

0992 ⇢ **Mirko Ilić Corp.**
⇢ USA

0993 ⇢ **Regan Blough**
⇢ USA

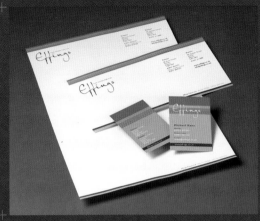

0994 ⇢ **biz-R**
⇢ UK

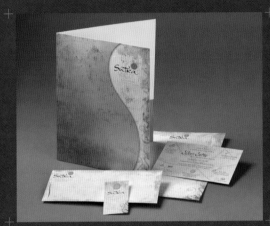

0995 ⇢ **On The Edge Design, Inc**
⇢ USA

0996 ⇢ **On The Edge Design, Inc**
⇢ USA

0997 ⇢ **On The Edge Design, Inc**
⇢ USA

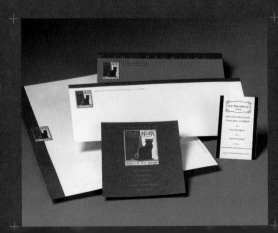

07

CHAPTER 6
END MATTER

28 Limited Brand
Bessemerstrasse 85, Halle 8
44793 Bochum
Germany
+49 (0) 234 91 609 51
www.twenty-eight.de

0189, 0190, 0191
Art Director/Designer: Mirco Kurth
Client: Maluma

804© Graphic Design
Ronsdorfer Strasse 77a
40233 Düsseldorf
Germany
+49 (0) 211 77 92 760
www.achtnullvier.de

0420, 0472, 0473, 0474, 0475, 0735,
0770, 0901
Art Directors/Designers: Helge Dirk
Rieder, Oliver Henn
Client: Mielert's

A1.0 Design
Rua Helena, 170
4º Andar
Vila Olímpia
São Paulo SP
Brazil
+55 (11) 3845 3503
www.a10.com.br

0063, 0064, 0080, 0514, 0515
Art Director: Margarete Takeda
Designer: Maria Costa Lino
Client: A Bela Sintra

AdamsMorioka
8484 Wilshire Blvd., Suite 600
Beverly Hills, CA 90211
USA
323-966-5990
www.adamsmorioka.com

0100, 0101, 0219, 0535, 0910
Art Director/Designer: Noreen Morioka
Client: Nic's

0115, 0989
Art Directors/Designers: Sean Adams,
Noreen Morioka
Client: Theater Square Grill

0125, 0340, 0481, 0749
Art Directors/Designers: Sean Adams,
Noreen Morioka
Client: Fusion at PDC

0286, 0432, 0750
Art Directors/Designers: Sean Adams,
Noreen Morioka
Client: Encounter

Adrienne Weiss Corporation
c/o The Levy Restaurants
980 N Michigan Ave.
Suite 400
Chicago, IL 60611
USA

0603
Client: DIVE! Los Angeles and DIVE! Las
Vegas (The Levy Restaurants/Steven
Spielberg and Jeffrey Katzenberger)

Advance Design Center
2501 Oak Lawn Ave., Suite 200
Dallas, TX 75219
USA
214-526-1420
www.adc-inc.com

0205
Art Director/Designer: Doug Livingston
Client: Georgie's Chow House

0207
Art Director: Doug Livingston
Designer: Jesus Acosta
Client: Pollo Campero

0208
Art Director: Doug Livingston
Designer: Christine Pasienski
Client: Ravelo's Pastaria

0240
Art Director: Doug Livingston
Designer: Christine Pasienski
Client: Milano's

Adventure Advertising
PO Box 576
Camden, ME 04843
USA

0651
Art Director/Designer: Joseph Ryan
Illustrator: Jerry Sterman
Client: Sea Dog Brewing Company

Alexander Design Associates
8 West 19th St.
Suite 2A
New York, NY 10011
USA
212-807-6641

0153
Art Director: Dean Alexander
Designer: Kelly Tamaki
Client: Restaurant Associates (Tropica
Caribbean Seafood)

Allies
108 Great Portland St.
London W1W 6PG
UK
+44 0 20 7636 3377
www.alliesdesign.com

0504, 0505, 0506
Art Director: Susanna Cook
Designer: Colin Smith
Client: Kyle Cathie Publishers Ltd

0507, 0508
Art Director: Susanna Cook
Designer: Amy Joyce
Client: B@1

Annabelle Wimer Design
539 Polk Blvd.
Suite B
Des Moines, IA 50312
USA
515-255-4953

0626
Art Director/Designer: Annabel Wimer
Client: Steve Villmain (The Diner)

The Art Commission Inc.
2287 Capehart Cir. NE
Atlanta, GA 30345
USA
404-636-9149

0171
Art Director: Bruce Phillips
Designer: Cynthia Virkler
Illustrator: Bruce Phillips, Cynthia Virkler
Client: Shelia Thacker (Thames Street
Tavern)

Art Institute of California, Orange County
3601 West Sunflower Ave.
Santa Ana, CA 92704
USA
Mailing address: 10 Thunder Run 6-d
Irvine, CA 92614, USA
949-551-5662
www.artinstitutes.edu/orangecounty
atiragram3@hotmail.com

0231
Art director: Maggie Vazquez, MFA
Designer: J-R Ignacio
Client: A-Sushi

0248
Art Director: Maggie Vazquez, MFA
Designer: Simson Chanta
Client: Tres Hermanos

Artie Horowitz Design
632 South Highland Ave.
Los Angeles, CA 90036
USA

0681
Designer: Artie Horowitz
Client: Maria's Cucina (Boris Brezinger)

Associates Design
3177 MacArthur Blvd.
Northbrook, IL 60062
USA

0518
Art Director: Chuck Polonsky
Designer: Beth Finn
Client: Banners, FleetCenter Boston
(Sportservice)

0559
Art Director: Chuck Polonsky
Designer: Bobbie Serafini
Illustrator: Jill Arena
Client: Allie's American Grille (Marriott
Hotels)

0560
Art Director: Chuck Polonsky
Designer/Illustrator: Shirley Bonk
Client: Marriott Philadelphia Airport

0599
Art Director: Chuck Polonsky
Designer/Illustrator: Jill Arena
Client: Oceana (Marriott Hotels)

0621, 0622, 0623
Art Director: Chuck Polonsky
Designer: Jill Arena
Photographer: Dave Slavinski
Computer Artist: John Arena
Client: All Seasons Café (Hyatt Hotels
Corp.)

0642
Art Director: Chuck Polonsky
Designer: Beth Finn
Client: Grand Hyatt (Humu Humu)

0643
Art Director: Chuck Polonsky
Designer/Illustrator: Jill Arena
Client: Sportservice

0654
Art Director: Chuck Polonsky
Designer/Illustrator: Mary Greco
Client: Legends, FleetCenter Boston
(Sportservice)

0655, 0664
Art Director: Chuck Polonsky
Designer/Illustrator: Jill Arena
Client: Prairie Knights Casino (Seven
Circles)

0663
Art Director: Chuck Polonsky
Designer/Illustrator: Roberta Serafini
Client: Hyatt Orlando Airport
(Hemisphere)

Ayse Çelem Design
Birinci Cadde No. 89
Arnavutköy
Istanbul 34345
Turkey
+90 0212 358 20 93
www.aysecelemdesign.com

0414, 0415, 0416, 0953
Art Director/Designer: Ayse Çelem
Client: Ulus 29 Restaurant

Bakken Creative Co.
1250 Addison, Studio 208
Berkeley, CA 94702
USA
510-540-8260
www.bakkencreativeco.com

0449, 0769
Art Director: Michelle Bakken
Designer: Jennifer Chan
Client: Firefly, Kimpton Group

0476
Art Director: Michelle Bakken
Designer: Gina Mondello
Client: South Water Kitchen, Kimpton
Group

0914, 0915, 0976, 0979
Art Director: Michelle Bakken
Designer: Gina Mondello
Client: Three Degrees, Larkspur
Hospitality

0975
Art Director: Michelle Bakken
Designer: Gina Mondello
Client: Bar Rouge, Kimpton Group

Bartosz Oczujda
ul. Włodkowica 3/5
Poznań Wielkopolska 60-334
Poland
+48 505 180 482
b9999@o2.pl

0843
Art Director/Designer: Bartosz Oczujda
Client: Pożegnanie z Afryką

BASELINE
Office 71, Stirling Business Centre
Stirling
FK8 2DZ Scotland
UK
+44 01786 430 378
www.selinegraphics.co.uk
b@selinegraphics.co.uk

0357, 0477
Art Director: Douglas Walker
Designer: Steven Bonner
Client: Maclay Inns

0859
Art Director: Douglas Walker
Designer: Steven Bonner
Client: Conran Restaurants

Betty Soldi
29 Sheen Common Dr.
Richmond, Surrey
TW10 5BW
UK

1.000
Designer: Betty Soldi
Client: Arts Theatre Café (Phil Owens, Jo Phillips)

BigEyes Design
31 Rothschild Blvd., Room 35
Tel Aviv 66883
Israel
+972 54 530 7229
lehav@bigeyes.co.il
bigeyes.express@gmail.com

0096, 0097, 01.88, 021.3, 0251, 0494, 0495, 0496, 0497, 0498, 0499, 0500, 0501, 0502, 0503, 0534, 0536, 0537, 0538, 0539, 0542, 0696, 0697, 0700, 0802, 0804
Art Director/Designer: Lahav Halevy
Client: R2M Corporation

biz-R
35A Fore St.
Totnes, Devon TQ95HN
UK
+44 01803 868989
www.biz-r.co.uk
retail@biz-r.co.uk

0422, 0423, 0685, 0725, 0785, 0994
Art Director: Blair Thomson
Designer: Tish England
Client: Effings

bonbon london
F5, 13 The Paragon
London
UK
+44 07932 008 225
www.bonbonlondon.com
studio@bonbonlondon.com

01.02, 0254, 041.2, 0709, 0796, 081.6, 081.7, 0924, 0925, 0956, 0957, 0958, 0960
Art Directors: Mark Harper, Sasha Castling
Designer: Mark Harper
Client: Jill Bartlett & Company

01.04, 01.45, 0255, 0520, 0585, 0734, 0774, 0834, 0922
Art Directors: Mark Harper, Sasha Castling
Designer: Mark Harper
Client: Cafeteria 124

0371, 041.9, 0450, 0457, 0458, 0459, 0524, 0682, 0687, 0688, 0689, 071.9, 0795, 081.4, 081.5, 0871, 0877, 0878, 0905, 0946, 0949
Art Directors: Mark Harper, Sasha Castling
Designer: Mark Harper
Client: Smiths of Smithfield

Bowhaus Design Groupe
340 North 12th St., Suite 314
Philadelphia, PA 19107
USA
215-733-0603
www.bowhausdesign.com
info@bowhausdesign.com

0238, 0941
Art Director: Matt O'Rourke
Designer: Matt Labul
Client: MilkBoy Coffee

0276
Art Director/Designer: Matt O'Rourke
Client: Fiso

Brandhouse WTS
10A Frederick Close
London W2 2HD
UK
+44 020 7262 1707
www.brandhouse.co.uk/flash.html
kj@brandhousewts.com

0061, 01.1.0, 0252, 0493
Art Director: Dave Beard
Designer: Bronwen Edwards
Client: Mitchells and Butlers

0081, 0082, 0492, 051.3, 0772, 0806, 0807, 0810
Art Director: Dave Beard
Designer: Bronwen Edwards
Client: 43 South Molton Street

021.5, 051.1
Art Director: Dave Beard
Designer: Keely Jackman
Client: Mitchells and Butlers

051.2
Art Director: Dave Beard
Designer: Mel Maynard
Client: Mitchells and Butlers

0531
Art Director: Dave Beard
Designer: Emma Staveacre
Client: Mitchells and Butlers

Braue Strategic Brand Design
Eiswerkestrasse 8
27572 Bremerhaven
Germany
+49 0471 983 82 0
www.braue.info

01.47, 0269, 0522, 0831, 0952
Art Director/Designer: Marçel Robbers
Client: Restaurant Leuchtfeuer

0391, 051.9, 0786
Art Director: Kai Braue
Designers: Marçel Robbers, Sandra Blum
Client: Caffè Bene

Bright & Associates
901 Abbot Kinney Blvd.
Venice, CA 90291
USA

0662, 0723
Art Directors: Bill Corridori, Keith Bright
Designer/Illustrator: Bill Corridori
Client: Gratis Restaurant

Bullet Communications Inc.
200 South Midland Ave.
Joliet, IL 60435
USA

Designer: Tim Scott
Client: Stella D'Italia Restaurant

0297, 0648
Designer: Tim Scott
Client: Pizza Picasso

Campus Collection
PO Box 2904
Tuscaloosa, AL 35403
USA
205-758-0678
www.campuscollection.net

0202, 0896
Art Director: Joe Rossomanno
Designer: Phillip Sanford
Client: Starlite Diner

0341
Art Director: Joe Rossomano
Designer: Courtney Dagenhart
Client: Keys Fisheries

0342
Art Director: Joe Rossomano
Designer: Tony Brock
Client: Sam's Corner

0390
Designer: Tony Brock
Client: Rosie's Tamale House

0881
Art Director: Joe Rossomano
Designer: Lulu Kaufman
Client: Blue Heaven

0883
Art Director: Joe Rossomano
Designer: Debbie Lewis
Client: Cuban Rooster

0885
Art Director: Joe Rossomano
Designer: Larry McAfee
Client: Bumpers

0887
Art Director: Joe Rossomano
Designer: Pam Bullington
Client: Frostbites

0889
Art Director: Joe Rossomano
Designers: Pam Bullington, Neal Cross
Client: Hello Deli

0891
Art Director: Joe Rossomano
Designer: Pam Bullington
Client: Pat O'Brien's

0894
Art Director/Designer: Joe Rossomano
Client: Mad Hatter's

0895
Art Director: Joe Rossomano
Designer: Debbie Lewis
Client: Conch Republic

CDI Studios
2215-A Renaissance Dr.
Las Vegas, NV 89119
USA
702-876-3316
www.cdistudios.com

0236, 0897
Art Director: Dan McElhattan III
Illustrator: David Araujo
Client: Bleu Gourmet

0281
Art Director/Designer: Dan McElhattan III
Client: Osaka Sushi Bar

0293, 0876
Art Director: Dan McElhattan III
Designers: Dan McElhattan III, David Araujo
Client: Gasoline Alley

0316
Art Director/Designer: Dan McElhattan III
Client: Northside Nathan's

0324, 0674
Art Director: Victoria Hart
Designer: Brian Felgar
Client: Julie Anne's Bakery, Café & Fine Foods

0325
Art Director: Dan McElhattan III
Designers: Dan McElhattan III, Alfred Herczeg

Chris Rooney Illustration/Design
1317 Santa Fe Ave.
Berkeley, CA 94702
USA
415-827-3729
looneyrooney@mindspring.com

0764
Designer: Chris Rooney
Client: Tastings

christiansen: creative
511 2nd St., Suite 203
Hudson, WI 54016
USA
715-381-8480
www.christiansencreative.com

0062, 0105, 0470, 0471, 0555, 0902
Art Directors/Designers: Dave MacDonald, Tricia Christiansen
Client: Bricks Neapolitan Pizza

Coco Raynes Graphics, Inc.
35 Newbury St.
Boston, MA 02116
USA
617-536-9052

0683
Art Director: Coco Raynes
Designers: Coco Raynes, Brian Erickson
Client: Lou Lou's Rotisserie

Commarts, Inc.
1112 Pearl St.
Boulder, CO 80302
USA
303-447-8202
www.commartsdesign.com

0193, 0344
Art Director/Designer: Mark Jasin
Client: Cortex Companies

0294
Art Director: Richard Foy
Designer: Jeff Keil
Client: Laudisio's Restaurant

Corbin Design
109 East Front St. #304
Traverse City, MI 49684
USA
616-947-1236

0636
Art Director: Jeffry Corbin
Designer: Janet Mortensen
Client: Joe Bologna (Rookies Clubhouse)

Crush Design and Art Direction
6 Gloucester St.
Brighton BN1 4EW
UK
+44 0 1273 60 60 58
www.crushed.co.uk
contact@crushed.co.uk

0094, 0427, 0801, 0819, 0986
Art Director: Carl Rush
Designers: Tim Diacon, Chris Pelling,
Simon Slater
Client: Scoundrels Ltd

0249, 0425, 0426
Art Director: Carl Rush
Designer: Simon Slater
Client: Medicine Group

CWA Inc.
4015 Ibis St.
San Diego, CA 92103
USA
619-299-0431

0741
Art Director/Illustrator: Susan Merritt
Designer: Christy Van Deman
Client: Koll International (La Paloma at
Palmilla)

Damion Hickman Design
1760 Kaiser Ave.
Irvine, CA 92614
USA
949-261-7857
www.damionhickman.com

0032, 0146
Art Director: Damion Hickman
Designer: Leighton Hubbell
Client: Ten Restaurant

0333
Art Director: Damion Hickman
Designer: Colin Freeman
Client: Sutra Lounge

0337
Art Director: Damion Hickman
Designer: Leighton Hubbell
Client: Ten Restaurant

0338
Art Director: Damion Hickman
Designer: Leighton Hubbell
Client: Tentation

0356
Art Director: Damion Hickman
Designer: Billi Rakov
Client: Blush Lounge

David Carter Design
4112 Swiss Ave.
Dallas, TX 75204
USA

0582, 0583
Art Director: Lori Wilson
Designers: Lori Wilson, Gary Lobue, Jr.
Client: Spike's Jazz Bar (Hotel Principe
Felipe)

0647
Designer: Sharon LeJeune
Client: Anzu

David Caunce
67 Acres Rd.
Chorlton
Manchester M21 9EB
UK
+44 0161 861 9309
www.imagine-cga.co.uk

0332, 0349, 0451, 0452, 0453, 0454,
0455, 0675, 0676, 0677, 0701, 0702,
0824, 0872, 0955
Art Director/Designer: David Caunce
Client: The Bean Counter

Dean Johnson Design
646 Massachusetts Ave.
Indianapolis, IN 46250
USA
317-634-8020
www.deanjohnson.com

0303
Art Director: Mike Schwab
Designers: Mike Schwab, Bruce Dean
Client: Mo'Joe Coffeehouse

0317
Art Director/Designer: Mike Schwab
Client: Loughmiller's Pub & Eatery

0618
Designers: Mike Schwab, Bruce Dean
Client: Some Guys Pizza

The Design Laboratory
The Design Laboratory at the
Innovation Center
Central Saint Martins College of Art
and Design
Southampton Row
London WC1B 4AP
UK
+44 0 20 7514 7028
www.designlaboratory.co.uk

0404, 0405, 0406, 0407, 0408, 0670,
0907, 0909, 0962, 0983, 0984
Art Directors: Brent Richards, Yann
Mathias
Designers: Milos Covic, Eva Helberger
Client: The Fat Duck Restaurant

Disney Design Group
Walt Disney World
PO Box 10,000
Lake Buena Vista, FL 32830-1000
USA

0554
Art Directors: Jeff Morris,
Renee Schneider
Designer: Mimi Palladino
Illustrator: Michael Mohjer
Writer: Tony Fernandez
Client: Bonfamille's Café (Disney's
Port Orleans Resort)

0596, 0611
Art Directors: Jeff Morris,
Renee Schneider
Designers: Thomas Scott,
Michael Mohjer
Illustrator: Michael Mohjer
Client: Crockett's Tavern (Disney's Fort
Wilderness Resort)

0613
Art Directors: Jeff Morris,
Renee Schneider
Designer: Mimi Palladino
Illustrator: Michael Mohjer
Writer: Tony Fernandez
Client: Whispering Canyon Café
(Disney's Wilderness Lodge)

0615
Art Directors: Jeff Morris, Renee
Schneider
Designer: Mimi Palladino
Illustrator: Peter Emslie
Client: Narcoosee's (Disney's Grand
Floridian Beach Resort)

Dornig Graphic Design
Saegerstrasse 4
A-6850 Dornbirn
Austria
0043 664 1438374
dornig@saegenvier.at

0221, 0222, 0781, 0862
Art Director/Designer: Kurt Dornig
Client: Theater Café

Ducks Design
Goetheallee 19
22765 Hamburg
Germany
+49 40 38083889
www.ducksdesign.de
contact@ducksdesign.de

0265, 0379
Art Director/Designer: Ray Nher
Client: Events Promotion EPA

0270
Art Director/Designer: Ray Nher
Client: Titanic

0331, 0743, 0870, 0981
Art Director/Designer: Kay Penndorf
Client: Realto

0355, 0544, 0545, 0547, 0805
Art Director/Designer: Ray Nher
Client: Trips'e Bock

The Dunlavey Studio
3576 McKinley Blvd.
Suite 200
Sacramento, CA 95816
USA
916-451-2170

0068
Art Director/Designer: Michael Dunlavey
Client: Java City at Market Square

0123, 0158, 0159, 0160
Art Director/Designer: Michael Dunlavey
Client: Jeff Tay (Fabulous 50's Café)

DZ6 Design
Av. Nova York, No. 294, Casa 1
Porto Alegre RS 90550-070
Brazil
+55 51 3342 2725
www.dz6.com.br
dz6@dz6.com.br

0439, 0912
Art Director/Designer: Janine Moura
Client: Constantino Café

Eilts Anderson Tracy
4111 Baltimore
Kansas City, MO 64111
USA
816-931-2687

0657
Art Director/Designer/Illustrator:
Patrice Eilts
Client: PB&J Restaurants (Coyote Grill)

Elephant Design Pvt. Ltd.
13, Kumar Srushti
Bavdhan
Pune, Maharashtra, 411 021
India
+91 20 22951059
www.elephantdesign.com

0034, 0103, 0398
Art Directors: Ashwini Deshpande,
Ashish Deshpande
Designers: Sheetal, Nitin
Client: Hindustan Lever Limited

Elfen
20 Harrowby Lane
Cardiff Bay
Cardiff CF10 5GN
Wales
+44 0 29 2048 4824
www.elfen.co.uk
post@elfen.co.uk

0070, 0835
Art Director: Guto Evans
Designer: Matthew James
Client: Armless Dragon

0076, 0149
Art Director: Guto Evans
Designer: Wayne Harris
Client: Café Junior

Emma Main
PO Box 11-331 Wellington
Harcourts Building, Suite 316
22 Grey St.
New Zealand

0667
Designer/Illustrator: Emma Main
Photographer: Kerry MacKay
Typesetter: Alistair Best
Signage Sculptors: Andrew "Floppy"
Beattie, Peter Hutchinson
Client: Mondo Cucina, Wellington,
New Zealand

Etc Deseño Gráfico
CC Las Tapias, Nivel 2 Local
14 Mérida
Venezuela
Mailing address: Urb La Mara
Calle 5 Qta. Ta'lluvia
Mérida
Venezuela 5101
+58 414 7456416
biancaprado@gmail.com

0180
Art Director: Bianca Prado
Designers: Bianca Prado, Luisa Prado
Client: Food Planet

0247
Art Director: Bianca Prado
Designers: Bianca Prado, Luisa Prado
Client: Rudy's Pizza

Evenson Design Group
4445 Overland Ave.
Culver City, CA 90230
USA
310-204-1995
www.evensondesign.com
edgmail@evensondesign.com

0166
Art Director: Stan Evenson
Designer: John Lovause
Client: Cubby's Coffeehouse

0170
Art Director: Stan Evenson
Designer: Katja Loesch
Client: Synergy

0392, 0714, 0875
Art Directors: Stan Evenson, Mark Sojka
Designer: John Lovause
Client: Cubby's Coffeehouse

0397
Art Directors: Stan Evenson, Mark Sojka
Designer: Katja Loesch
Client: Synergy

0999
Art Directors: Stan Evenson, Mark Sojka
Designer: Katja Loesch
Client: Synergy

EyeSpeak
235 S Main St., Suite A
Jonesboro, AR 72401
USA
870-530-2541
www.eyespeakvc.com

0291
Art Director/Designer: Kimberly Boyd
Vickrey
Client: Club Luna

0299
Art Director/Designer: Kimberly Boyd
Vickrey
Client: Pieros

0302
Art Directors: Kimberly Boyd Vickrey,
Eric Vickrey
Designer: Lisa Carter
Client: Envisions Smelly Cat Shak

Fabrice Praeger
54 bis, rue de l'Érmitage
75020 Paris
France
01 60 33 17 00
fabrice.praeger@wanadoo.fr

0413, 0629, 0900, 0913, 0932, 0933,
0934
Art Director/Designer: Fabrice Praeger
Client: Tahiti/ Reflet/ La Petite Épicerie

Finest/Magma Brand Design
Südendstr. 52
76135 Karlsruhe
Germany
+49 721 831.422 0
www.finestmagma.com
info@finestmagma.com

0065, 0095, 0259, 0261, 0435, 0773
Art Director/Designer: Lars Harmsen
Client: Café Bar 53

0273, 0274, 0277, 0541, 0751, 0752,
0789, 0790, 0791
Art Director: Lars Harmsen
Designers: Sandra Augstein, Ulrich Weiß
Client: G. Braun Verlag

FITCH
1266 Manning Parkway
Powell, OH 43065
USA
614-885-3453
www.fitch.com

0051, 0052, 0053
Art Director: Brian Harvey
Designer: Bill Weikart
Client: Taberna del Tequila, Sky Harbor

0055, 0056, 0057
Art Director: Brian Harvey
Designer: Bill Weikart
Client: Expedia Café

0058, 0067
Art Director: David Denniston
Designer: Paul Teeples
Client: Caribou Coffee

0059, 0060
Art Director: Brian Harvey
Designer: Bill Weikart
Client: Pei Wei Asian Diner

0072
Art Director: Brian Harvey
Designer: Bill Weikart
Client: Chef Jimmy's

Fresh Oil
251 Cottage St.
Pawtucket, RI 02860
USA
401-709-4656
www.freshoil.com

0263
Art Director/Designer: Dan Stebbings
Client: 22 Bowen's

0305
Art Director/Designer: Dan Stebbings
Client: Ollie's Noodle Shop & Grille

0308
Art Director/Designer: Dan Stebbings
Client: Cowesett Inn

0309, 0813
Art Director: Dan Stebbings
Designers: Dan Stebbings, Nelson Couto
Client: PB's Diner

0312
Art Director: Dan Stebbings
Designers: Dan Stebbings, Nelson Couto
Client: Sonoma - California Café

0315, 0540, 0827
Art Director: Dan Stebbings
Designer: Nelson Couto
Client: Red Stripe - An American
Brasserie

0351
Art Director/Designer: Dan Stebbings
Client: XO Steakhouse

0352
Art Director: Dan Stebbings
Designer: Nelson Couto
Client: China Sky

0358, 0359
Art Director: Dan Stebbings
Designers: Dan Stebbings, Nelson Couto
Client: Madhouse Café

0372
Art Director/Designer: Dan Stebbings
Client: Siena - Tuscan Soul Food

0375, 0376
Art Director/Designer: Dan Stebbings
Client: Toù Bagaille

0543
Art Director/Designer: Dan Stebbings
Client: Café Newport

From Scratch Design Studio
1325 G St. NW, Suite 500
Washington, DC 20005
USA
202-449-7652
www.fromscratch.us

0220, 0491, 0942, 0943, 0982
Art Director/Designer: Cristian
Strittmatter
Client: Bezu (Eddie Benaim)

0264, 0478, 0738
Art Director/Designer: Cristian
Strittmatter
Client: Rasika (Knightsbridge
Management)

Frost Design, Sydney
Level 1, 15 Foster St.
Surry Hills, NSW 2010
Australia
+61 2 9280 4233
www.frostdesign.com.au

0049, 0050
Art Director: Vince Frost
Client: Sydney Dance Cafe

0138, 0866, 0867, 0868, 0919, 0920
Art Director: Vince Frost
Client: Nautilus Group (Coast Restaurant)

0525, 0526, 0527, 0528, 0812, 0918
Art Director: Vince Frost
Client: Nautilus Group (Manta Restaurant)

Fullblastinc.com
618 NW Glisan, #200
Portland, OR 97209
USA
503-227-2002
www.fullblastinc.com
design@fullblastinc.com

0154, 0556, 0830, 0882, 0950, 0951
Art Director/Designer: N. Todd Skiles
Client: Park Kitchen

0529
Art Director/Designer: N. Todd Skiles
Client: Blueplate

0241
Art Director/Designer: N. Todd Skiles
Client: Max's Fanno Creek Brew Pub

0530, 0533
Art Director/Designer/Photographer:
N. Todd Skiles
Client: Vita Café

Gabriel Kalach - Visual Communication
1000 West Ave., #1004
Miami Beach, FL 33139
USA
305-532-2336
proartgraphics@mac.com

0253
Art Director/Designer: Gabriel Kalach
Client: Arrso Restaurants

0256
Art Director/Designer: Gabriel Kalach
Client: 820 Gotham Bar

0262
Art Director/Designer: Gabriel Kalach
Client: 62 Bar Lounge

0311
Art Director/Designer: Gabriel Kalach
Client: Mas Allá Restaurant

0318
Art Director/Designer: Gabriel Kalach
Client: 820 Bar – Restaurant

0382
Art Director/Designer: Gabriel Kalach
Client: Mas Allá Restaurant

0383
Art Director/Designer: Gabriel Kalach
Client: Capisce? Restaurant

0384
Art Director/Designer: Gabriel Kalach
Client: Karu&Y

0385
Art Director/Designer: Gabriel
Kalach Karu&Y

0393
Art Director/Designer: Gabriel Kalach
Client: Gaira Café

Gingerbee Creative
44 N. Last Chance Gulch
Helena, MT 59601
USA
406-443-3032
www.gingerbee.com

0242
Designer: Ginger Knaff
Client: Moose Magoo's

Gloria Paul
150 W. Jefferson Ave.
Suite 100
Detroit, MI 48226
USA

0641, 0644
Designer: Gloria Paul
Client: Cup·A·Cino Coffee House
(Jennifer Bell)

Graphic Content
600 N Bishop Ave., Suite 200
Dallas, TX 75208
USA
214-948-6969
www.graphiccontent.com

0482
Art Director/Designer: Art Garcia
Client: Marie Gabrile

0483
Art Directors: Art Garcia, Jesus Nava
Designer: Josh Weatherspoon
Client: Campuzano Restaurant

0731
Art Director/Designer: Art Garcia
Client: Marie Gabrile

Graphicwise, Inc.
PO Box 53801
Irvine, CA 92619
USA
949-859-0767
www.graphicwise.com
info@graphicwise.com

0198, 0589, 0988
Art Director: Kevin Javid
Designer: Art Javid
Client: Pier39

Greiner Design Associates
3111 N. Ravenswood
Chicago, IL 60657
USA
312-404-0210

0043, 0045
Designer: John Greiner
Photographer: Hedrich/Blessing
Client: Art Institute of Chicago (Court Cafeteria)

Greteman Group
142 North Mosley
Wichita, KS 67202
USA

0168
Art Director: Sonia Greteman
Designers: Sonia Greteman, Jo Quillin, Chris Parks
Client: Oaxaca Grill

Hamagami/Carroll, Inc.
1316 3rd Street Promenade, Suite 305
Santa Monica, CA 90401
USA
310-458-7600

0116, 0117, 0119, 0120, 0124
Client: Disney

Hand Made Group
Via Sartori, 18
52017 Stia (AR)
Italy
+39 0575 582083
www.hmg.it

0194, 0267, 0574, 0575, 0825
Art Director: Alessandro Esteri
Designer: Davide Premuni
Client: La Tartine

Hans Flink Design Inc.
11 Martine Ave.
White Plains, NY 10606
USA
914-328-0888

0721, 0722
Designers: Hans D. Flink and staff
Client: Grand Central Oyster Bar &
Restaurant

Hansen Associates
11956 Bernardo Plaza Dr.
PMB159
San Diego, CA 92128-2538
USA
858-829-7954
ccarr@colleencarr.com

0209
Art Director: Ted Hansen
Designer: Colleen Carr
Client: Oasis Bar & Grill

Hardy Design
Rua Araguari 1541
5º Andar 30190-111
Belo Horizonte
Brazil
+55 31 3275 3095
www.hardydesign.com.br

0521, 0587, 0923, 0990
Art Director: Mariana Hardy
Designers: Andréa Gomes, Carolina
Marini, Mariana Hardy
Client: Café Fina Flor

Hat-Trick Design
3 Morollo St, Third Floor
London SE1 3HB
UK
+44 0 20 74037875
www.hat-trickdesign.co.uk

0046, 0047
Art Directors: David Kimpton, Jim
Sutherland, Gareth Howat
Designer: Ben Christie
Client: The Salvation Army

0048
Art Directors: David Kimpton, Jim
Sutherland, Gareth Howat
Designer: Alex Swatridge
Client: Xchanging

Heather Heflin
CAA Box 801
Bloomfield Hills, MI 48303
USA

0576, 0577
Designer: Heather Heflin
Client: Farah's on the Avenue (Nick
Farah)

Heinzle Design
1060 Vienna
Austria
+43 1 5860852
www.heinzledesign.at
office@heinzledesign.at

0272, 0548, 0564
Art Director: Lothar Aemilian Heinzle
Designer: Markus Maier
Client: Reflex

Hollis Brand Communications
680 West Beech St., Suite 1
San Diego, CA 92101
USA
619-234-2061
www.hollisbc.com

0086, 0150, 0161, 0517, 0590, 0591,
0778, 0792, 0809, 0944, 0945
Art Director/Designer: Don Hollis
Client: Chive

0118, 0550, 0793, 0828
Art Director/Designer: Don Hollis
Client: D-lush Deluxe Beverage Joint

0012, 0136, 0523, 0660, 0777, 0947,
0948, 0959, 0961, 0978, 0980
Art Director: Don Hollis
Designers: Don Hollis, Angela Villareal
Client: Jordan Restaurant

0784
Art Director: Don Hollis
Designers: Don Hollis, Angela Villareal
Client: Blanca Restaurant

0803, 0977
Art Director/Designer: Don Hollis
Client: Cendio

Hornall Anderson Design Works
710 2nd Ave., Suite 1300
Seattle, WA 98104
USA
206-826-2329
www.hadw.com

0033, 0553
Art Directors: Lisa Cerveny, James Tee,
Tiffany Place
Client: Tahitian Noni

0035, 0036, 0037, 0038, 0039, 0040,
0140, 0141, 0672, 0707, 0708, 0711,
0712, 0713, 0854
Art Director: Jack Anderson
Designers: James Tee, Sonja Max
Client: Terra Vida Coffee

0726, 0836, 0853
Art Directors: Jack Anderson,
Larry Anderson
Designers: Larry Anderson, Elmer
de la Cruz, Bruce Stigler, Jay Hilburn,
Dorothee Soechting, Don Stayner
Client: Widmer Brothers Brewery

0727, 0855, 0856
Art Directors: Jack Anderson,
Larry Anderson
Designers: Larry Anderson, Elmer de la
Cruz, Bruce Stigler, Jay Hilburn, Bruce
Branson-Meyer
Client: Widmer Brothers Brewery

0728, 0852
Art Directors: Jack Anderson,
Bruce Stigler
Designers: Larry Anderson, Elmer de la
Cruz, Bruce Stigler, Jay Hilburn
Client: Widmer Brothers Brewery

Hunt Weber Clark Associates

525 Brannan St.
Suite 302
San Francisco, CA 94107
USA

0164
Art Director/Designer/Illustrator:
Nancy Hunt-Weber
Client: Kimco Hotel and Restaurant
Management (Corona Bar & Grill)

0174
Art Director: Nancy Hunt-Weber
Designer: Gary Williams
Illustrators: Nancy Hunt-Weber, Gary
Williams
Client: Hawthorne Lane

i_d buero

Bismarkstrasse 67A
70197 Stuttgart
Germany
+49 (0) 711 636 8000
www.i-dbuero.de

0004, 0005, 0087, 0113, 0350, 0402,
0403, 0739, 0898, 0899, 0908, 0964,
0965, 0966
Art Director: Oliver A. Krimmel
Client: Rubirosa, Gensfleisch

Inaria

10 Plato Place
72-74 St Dionis Rd.
London SW6 4TU
UK
+44 0 20 7384 0904
www.inaria-design.com

0216, 0671, 0690, 0732, 0973
Art Directors: Andrew Thomas, Debora
Berardi
Designer: Anna Leaver
Client: Firezza

The Invisions Group Ltd.

4927 Auburn Ave.
Suite 100
Bethesda, MD 20814-2641
USA

0169, 0395
Art Director: John Cabot Lodge
Designers: Denise Sparhawk, Michael
Kraine
Client: Kinkead's (Robert Kinkead)

Jeff Fisher LogoMotives

PO Box 17155
Portland, OR 97217
USA
503-283-8673
www.fisherlogomotives.com

0204
Art Director/Designer: Jeff Fisher
Client: North Bank Café

0206
Art Director/Designer: Jeff Fisher
Client: Glo's Broiler

0211
Art Director/Designer: Jeff Fisher
Client: Balaboosta Delicatessen

0380
Art Director/Designer: Jeff Fisher
Client: La Patisserie

0598
Art Director: Todd Pierce
Designer/Illustrator: Jeff Fisher
Client: Indies

John & Orna Designs

27 Belsize Lane
Belsize Mews Studio
London NW3 5AS
UK
+44 020 7431 9116
www.johnandornadesigns.co.uk
mail@johnandornadesigns.co.uk

0562, 0569, 0570
Art Director/Designer: John & Orna
Designs
Client: Stephen Lawrence Charitable
Trust

0571, 0572, 0573
Art Director/Designer: John & Orna
Designs
Client: Private client

John Evans Design

2200 North Lamar #220
Dallas, TX 75023
USA

0612
Art Director: Troy Scillian
Designer/Illustrator: John Evans
Client: Pargo's (MBRK)

John Kneapler Design

48 West 21st St.
New York, NY 10010
212-463-9774

0162
Art Director: John Kneapler
Designers: John Kneapler, Matt
Waldman, Daymon Bruck
Client: Stephan Loffredo, Thalia Loffredo
(Zoë)

The Jones Group

342 Marietta St., Suite #3
Atlanta, GA 30313
USA
404-523-2606
www.thejonesgroup.com

0192, 0226
Art Director: Vicky Jones
Designer: Kendra Lively
Client: Cenitare Restaurant Group

0201
Art Director: Vicky Jones
Designer: Brody Boyer
Client: Old Edwards Hospitality Group

0225
Art Director: Vicky Jones
Designer: Chris Lowndes
Client: Cenitare Restaurant Group

0290
Art Director: Vicky Jones
Designer: Kendra Lively
Client: Cenitare Restaurant Group

0326
Art Director: Vicky Jones
Designer: Kendra Lively
Client: Old Edwards Hospitality Group

0327
Art Director: Vicky Jones
Designer: Chris Lowndes
Client: Cenitare Restaurant Group

0388
Art Director: Vicky Jones
Designer: Kendra Lively
Client: Fotos Group

Jonni
Markreien 33b
0554 Oslo
Norway
+47 905 18 186
www.bleed.no

0088, 0090, 0106, 0183, 0421, 0424
Art Director/Designer: Jonni
Client: Café Kaos

Kapp & Associates, Inc.
2729 Prospect Ave.
Cleveland, OH 44115
USA

0578
Art Director: Cathryn Kapp
Designers: Derek Oyen, Sally Biel
Client: Sammy's at the Arena

Kenneth Diseño
Miguel Treviño s/n Fábrica San Pedro,
Centro
Uruapan Michoacan 60000
Mexico
+52 452 523 1738
mail@kengraf.net

0089
Art Director: Kenneth Treviño
Designers: Kenneth Treviño, Minerva
Galván
Client: Sunset

0128, 0374
Art Director/Designer: Kenneth Treviño
Client: La Placita

0143, 0346
Art Director: Kenneth Treviño
Designers: Kenneth Treviño, Minerva
Galván
Client: Café La Pérgola

0144, 0366
Art Director/Designer: Kenneth Treviño
Client: Dennis Pizza

0197
Art Director: Kenneth Treviño
Designers: Kenneth Treviño,
Sheila Peña R.
Client: Miura Bar

0199
Art Director/Designer: Kenneth Treviño
Client: Texas BBQ

0306
Art Director/Designer: Kenneth Treviño
Client: La Fontana

0363
Art Director/Designer: Kenneth Treviño
Client: Pollo Carretas

0364
Art Director/Designer: Kenneth Treviño
Client: La Lupita

0365
Art Director/Designer: Kenneth Treviño
Client: Mr. Costillas

0367
Art Director: Kenneth Treviño
Designers: Kenneth Treviño, Minerva
Galván
Client: Aqui Nomas

0368
Art Director/Designer: Kenneth Treviño
Client: Hippos

0369
Art Director/Designer: Kenneth Treviño
Client: El Tope

Laguna College of Art and Design
2222 Laguna Canyon Rd.
Laguna Beach, CA 92651
USA
Mailing address: 10 Thunder Run, 6-d
Irvine, CA 92614
USA
949-551-5662
www.lagunacollege.edu
atiragram3@hotmail.com

0210
Art Director: Maggie Vazquez, MFA
Designer: Kelli Buescher
Client: Heaven Cafe

0243
Art Director: Maggie Vazquez, MFA
Designer: Jieva Mulokas
Client: Seafood Jieva's Place

Lance Anderson Design
22 Margrave Pl.
Studio 5
San Francisco, CA 94133
USA

0561
Client: California Café Restaurant Corp.
Designer: Lance Anderson

Laura Jacoby
501 S. 16th St., 4R
Philadelphia, PA 19146
USA

0860
Designer: Laura Jacoby
Client: Crimson Moon Coffeehouse
(Kara Williamson)

Les LaMotte Design
3002 Keating Court
Burnsville, MN 55337
USA
612-894-1879

0173
Art Director/Designer/Illustrator: Les
LaMotte
Client: Breakfast Ventures (Coyote
Café)

Let Her Press
Lorna Stovall Design
1088 Queen Anne Place
Los Angeles, CA 90019
USA
213-931-5984

0604
Art Directors/Designers: Lorna Stovall,
Heather Van Haaften
Client: L'Orfeo (Opus)

The Levy Restaurants
980 N. Michigan Ave.
Suite 400
Chicago, IL 60611
USA

0595
Creative Director: Marcy L. Young
Designer: Karen Hoey
Client: Terrace Club at Jacobs Field
(Cleveland Indians)

0602
Creative Director: Marcy L. Young
Designers: Marcy L. Young, Karen Hoey
Client: The Stadium Club, Mezzanine Box
Catering (Chicago Cubs)

0632
Creative Director/ Designer/Illustrator:
Marcy Lansing
Client: Stadium Club at Wrigley Field

0635
Creative Director/ Designer/Illustrator:
Marcy Lansing
Client: Bistro 110

0650
Creative Director: Marcy L. Young
Designers: Karen Hoey
Client: The Rotunda, Executive
Suites, Day of Event Menu (Portland
Trailblazers)

LM
33 Gresse St.
London W1T 1QU
UK
+44(0)20 7580 9252
www.lewismoberly.com

0227, 0436
Art Director: Mary Lewis
Designers: Bryan Clark, Benji Weidemann
Client: Grand Hyatt, Dubai

0235, 0680
Art Directors/Designers: Mary Lewis,
Sonja Frick, Hideo Akiba, Fiona V-Smith
Client: Grand Hyatt

0394, 0673
Art Director: Mary Lewis
Designer: Ann Marshall
Client: Grand Hyatt, Dubai

Lodge Design
7 S. Johnson Ave.
Indianapolis, IN 46219
USA
317-590-5355
www.lodgedesign.com
0260, 0429, 0880
Designer: Eric Kass
Client: Red Rock Roadhouse

0310, 0963
Designer: Eric Kass
Client: Claddagh Irish Pub

Loewy
147 Grosvenor Rd.
London SW1V 3JY
UK
+44 0 020 7798 2000
www.loewygroup.com

0445, 0446, 0447, 0448
Art Director/Designer: Paul Burgess
Client: Signature

Lorenza Zanni
Via Avanzini 17
41100 Modena
Italy
+39 059 2928012
doppiazeta@libero.it

0279
Art Director/Designer: Lorenza Zanni
Client: Shibuya

Louise Fili Ltd.
71 Fifth Ave.
New York, NY 10003
USA

0744
Designer: Louise Fili
Client: Espace

Mark Frankel Design, Inc.
479 Newport Dr.
Naperville, IL 60565
USA
630-717-7630
www.markfrankeldesign.com

0282, 0319, 0329, 0434, 0437, 0440
Art Director: Kirsten Mentley
Designer: Mark Frankel
Client: Levy Restaurants

Marve Cooper Design, Ltd.
2120 W. Grand
Chicago, IL 60612
USA

0155, 0666
Art Director: Marve Cooper
Designers: Keith Curtis, Marve Cooper
Client: Tapas Barcelona (Restaurant
Development Group)

Mary Hutchison Design LLC
4010 Whitman Ave. N
Seattle, WA 98103
USA
206-407-3460
www.maryhutchisondesign.com
info@maryhutchisondesign.com

0129, 0268, 0565, 0987
Art Director/Designer: Mary Chin
Hutchison
Client: O'Asian Bistro, Inc.

McCord Graphic Design
Contact information not available
0489
Art Director/Designer: Walter McCord
Illustrators: Charles Loupot, Bud Hixson
Clients: Joanne Deitrich, Bim Deitrich
(Deitrich's in the Cresent)

0661
Art Director/Designer/Illustrator:
Walter McCord
Client: Kathy Cary, Will Cary (Lilly's)

The Menu Workshop
2815 Second Ave. #393
Seattle, WA 98121
USA
206-443-9516

0433
Art Director/Designer: Liz Kearney
Illustrator: Debbie Hanley
Client: J.J. Fryes

Milton Glaser, Inc.
207 E. 32nd St.
New York, NY 10016
USA
212-889-3161
www.miltonglaser.com
studio@miltonglaser.com

0027, 0028, 0029, 0030
Client: Stony Brook University

Mimolimit
Studio Najbrt
Fráni Šrámka 15
Praha 5
150 00 Czech Republic
+420 257 561060
www.najbrt.cz
studio@najbrt.cz

0026, 0108, 0109, 0485, 0486, 0487,
0488
Art Director: Aleš Najbrt
Designer: Bohumil Vašák
Client: Saxo Consulting
0163, 0430, 0766, 0767
Art Director/Designer: Aleš Najbrt
Client: DJ Svět, SVO

0178, 0431, 0720
Art Director: Aleš Najbrt
Designer: Zuzana Ledhická
Client: Targa Consulting

Mind's Eye Studio
PO Box 194
East Kelowna, BC V0H 1G0
Canada

0656, 0658
Art Director/Designer: Valery Mercer
Illustrator: Michael Downs
Client: Bailey's

Minelli, Inc.
381 Congress St.
Boston, MA 02210
USA
617-426-5343
www.minelli.com
webmail@minelli.com

0111, 0112, 0377, 0400
Art Director: Margarita Barrios Ponce
Designer: Stephen Rowe
Client: Oxford Street Grill

Mirko Ilić Corp.
207 East 32nd St.
New York, NY 10016
USA
212-481-9737
www.mirkoilic.com
studio@mirkoilic.com

**0130, 0131, 0132, 0417, 0456, 0737,
0754, 0755, 0756, 0757, 0758, 0759,
0760, 0761, 0762, 0968**
Art Director: Mirko Ilić
Designers: Mirko Ilić, Clint Shaner
Client: Le Cirque

0730, 0763, 0765, 0992
Art Director: Mirko Ilić
Designers: Mirko Ilić, Clint Shaner
Client: Summit

Mixer
Löwenplatz 5
CH-6004 Lucerne
Switzerland
+41 41 410 35 35
www.mixer.ch

0387, 0592, 0851
Art Director/Designer: Erich Brechbühl
Client: Wirtschaft zur Schlacht

Morrow McKenzie Design
322 NW 5th Ave., Suite 313
Portland, OR 97209
USA
503-222-0331
www.morrowmckenzie.com

0214, 0428
Art Director/Designer: Elizabeth
Morrow McKenzie
Client: Carafe Restaurant

Nita B. Creative
991 Selby Ave.
St. Paul, MN 55104
USA
651-644-2889
www.nitabcreative.com

0771
Art Director/Designer: Renita
Breitenbucher
Client: Thirst

Northern Artisan
PO Box 187
Rockwood, ME 04478
USA
207-534-2287

0842
Art Director: Jane Perry
Designer: Greg Donnelly
Client: Roadkill Café

Octavo Design Pty Ltd
11 Yarra St.
South Melbourne, Victoria, 3205
Australia
+61 3 9686 4703
www.octavodesign.com.au
info@octavodesign.com.au

0283, 0484, 0970
Art Director/Designer: Gary Domoney
Client: Da Vinci's

0300, 0480, 0971
Art Director/Designer: Gary Domoney
Client: Indulge

0301, 0972
Art Director/Designer: Gary Domoney
Client: Verve

0323, 0832, 0967
Art Director/Designer: Gary Domoney
Client: Kanela

Oliver Russell
217 South 11th St.
Boise, ID 83702
USA
208-287-6528
www.oliverrussell.com

0289
Art Directors: Tony Robin, Paul Carew
Designer: Tony Robin
Client: Franco Latino Restaurant

0328
Art Director: Paul Carew
Designer: Colleen Cahill
Client: Mortimer's Restaurant

On The Edge Design, Inc.
1601 Dove St., #294
Newport Beach, CA 92660
USA
949-251-0025
www.ontheedgedesign.com
info@ontheedgedesign.com

0370, 0929, 0930, 0931
Art Director: Gina Mims
Designers: Charissa Armenta, Leny
Evangelista
Client: The Lost Bean Organic
Coffee & Tea

0557, 0996
Art Directors: Gina Mims, Jeff Gasper
Designer: Melanie Fujita
Client: Honolulu Harry's Island Getaway

0558, 0997
Art Directors: Gina Mims, Jeff Gasper
Designer: Melanie Fujita
Client: The Lazy Dog Café

0605, 0775, 0797, 0798, 0995
Art Directors: Gina Mims, Jeff Gasper
Designer: Melanie Fujita
Client: Sutra Lounge

0653
Art Director: Joe Mozdzen
Designer/Illustrator: Jeff Gasper
Client: The Rex

0783, 0788, 0808, 0998
Art Director: Jeff Gasper
Designer: Tracey Lamberson
Client: Chat Noir Bistro & Jazz Lounge

0879, 0884, 0886, 0888, 0892, 0893,
Art Director/Designer: Gina Mims
Client: Yogurt Mill

Pentagram Design
204 Fifth Ave.
New York, NY 10010
USA

0073, 0092, 0624, 0625, 0746
Art Director: Michael Bierut
Designers: Michael Bierut, Lisa Cerveny
Illustrator: Woody Pirtle
Photographer: Reven TC Wurman
Client: Gotham Equities (The Good Diner)

0091, 0167
Art Directors: Michael Bierut (graphics),
James Biber (interiors)
Designer: Emily Hayes
Photographer: Peter Mauss/Esto
Client: Route 66 Roadhouse & Dining
Saloon (George Korten, Martin Winkler,
Kent Selig)

0552
Art Directors: Paula Scher (graphics),
James Biber (interiors)
Designer: Ron Louie
Photographer: Peter Mauss (Esto)
Client: One Fifth Avenue (Jerome
Kretchmer)

Ph.D
1524A Cloverfield Blvd.
Santa Monica, CA 90404
USA
310-829-0900
www.phdla.com

0232
Art Directors: Michael Hodgson, Clive
Piercy
Deigner: Michael Hodgson
Client: Bergamot Café

Poulin & Morris
286 Spring St., Sixth Floor
New York, NY 10013
USA
212-675-1332
www.poulinmorris.com
info@poulinmorris.com

0093, 0399, 0969
Designers: Richard Poulin, Brian Brindisi,
Anna Crider
Client: Dahesh Museum of Art

PM Design
11 Maple Terrace
Verona, NJ 07044
USA

0637
Art Director/Designer: Philip Marzo
Photographer: Geoff Reed
Client: Marion Scotto

PPA Design Limited
11 Macdonnell Rd. D-3
Midlevels
Hong Kong

0616, 0617
Art Director: Byron Jacobs
Designers: Byron Jacobs, Bernard Cau
Client: Cathay Pacific Airways

0638, 0668, 0669
Art Director: Byron Jacobs
Designers: Byron Jacobs, Tracy Hoi
Photographer: Ka Sing Lee
Client: Cathay Pacific Airways

0640
Art Director: Byron Jacobs
Designers: Byron Jacobs, Don FUnk
Illustrator: Brian Grimwood
Client: Dragon Airlines

Prejean Creative
305 La Rue France, Suite 200
Lafayette, LA 70508
USA
337-593-9051
www.prejeancreative.com

0244
Art Director/Designer: Kevin Prejean
Client: Lafayette Convention and
Visitors Commission

0245
Art Directors: Kevin Prejean, Gary LoBue
Designer: Gary LoBue
Client: Evangeline Downs Racetrack
& Casino

0246
Art Directors: Kevin Prejean, Gary LoBue
Designers: Mindi Nash, Kevin Prejean
Client: Evangeline Downs Racetrack &
Casino

0285, 0606, 0607, 0608, 0609
Art Directors: Kevin Prejean, Gary LoBue
Designer: Kevin Prejean
Client: Evangeline Downs Racetrack
& Casino

Public
10 Arkansas St., Suite L
San Francisco, CA 94107
USA
415-863-2541
www.publicdesign.com

0460, 0462, 0935, 0936, 0937, 0938,
0939, 0940
Art Director: Todd Foreman
Designers: Todd Foreman, Tessa Lee,
Nancy Thomas, Lindsay Wheeler
Client: Café Lo Cubano

0461, 0463, 0464, 0779, 0780, 0903
Art Director: Todd Foreman
Designer: Lindsay Wheeler
Client: Straits Restaurant

0465, 0466, 0467, 0532, 0748, 0904
Art Director: Todd Foreman
Designers: Todd Foreman, Tessa Lee,
Nancy Thomas, Lindsay Wheeler
Client: Bistro Vida

0468, 0469, 0479, 0684
Art Director: Todd Foreman
Designers: Todd Foreman, Tessa Lee,
Nancy Thomas, Lindsay Wheeler
Client: Sino

Q
Sonnenberger Str. 16
Wiesbaden 65193
Germany
+49 611 181310
info@a-home.de

0077, 0078, 0234
Art Director/Designer: Matthias Frey
Client: Blattgold Bar & Restaurant,
Hannover

0230
Art Director/Designer: Laurenz Nielbock
Client: Stiller's

0284
Art Director/Designer: Laurenz Nielbock
Client: L'Auberge

Qually & Company Inc.
2238 East Central St.
Evanston, IL 60201
USA
708-864-6316

01.57
Art Director: Robert Qually
Designer: Robert Qually, Holly Thomas,
Karla Walusiaki, Charles Sonties
Client: Windy City Café

R&Mag Graphic Design
Via del Pescatore 3
80053 Castellammare di Stabia
Italy
+39 081 8705053
www.remag.it
info@remag.it

0044, 0137, 0339
Art Directors/Designers: Fontanella, Di
Somma, Cesar
Client: Sapori D'Italia

0075, 0218, 0586
Art Directors/Designers: Fontanella, Di
Somma, Cesar
Client: Puldì

0133, 0829
Art Directors/Designers: Fontanella, Di
Somma, Cesar
Client: Sunshine

0139, 0271, 0686, 0811.
Art Directors/Designers: Fontanella, Di
Somma, Cesar
Client: The Wine Bar

0142, 0378, 0516
Art Directors/Designers: Fontanella, Di
Somma, Cesar
Client: Le Terrazze

0347, 0826
Art Directors/Designers: Fontanella, Di
Somma, Cesar
Client: Bar Di Martino

0588
Art Directors/Designers: Fontanella, Di
Somma, Cesar
Client: Vittó Pizza

Raidy Printing Group SAL
Postal Code 2071 3203
PO Box 175 165
Beirut
Lebanon
+961 156 7711
Mobile +961 323 4411
www.raidy.com
design@raidy.com

0229 , 0633, 0745
Art Director/Designer: Marie-Joe J.
Raidy
Client: Chantal Braidi

Raven Madd Design Company
PO Box 11.331 Wellington
Level 3 Harcourts Building
Corner Grey St. and Lambton Quay
New Zealand

0619
Art Director/Designer: Mark Curtis
Illustrators: Mark Curtis, Caroline
Campbell
Client: Chevy's (John Wiley)

Regan Blough
2112 W North Ave., Apt. 2W
Chicago, IL 60647
USA
773-227-3690
reganblough@sbcglobal.net

0320, 0724, 0736
Designer: Regan Blough
Client: The Smoke Daddy

0386, 0993
Art Director: Jilly Simons
Designer: Regan Todd
Client: D.O.C. Wine Bar

Re-Public
Laplandsgade 4
2300 Copenhagen S
Denmark
+45 4095 5180
www.re-public.com
emil@re-public.com

0224, 0818
Art Director/Designer: Emil Hartvig
Client: Hacienda

Restaurant Identity.com
62 Robbins Ave.
Berkeley Heights, NJ 07922
USA
903-665-6878

0266
Art Director: Philip Marzo
Designers: Philip Marzo, DeeDee
Burnside
Client: Sara Chea

0361
Art Director: Philip Marzo
Designers: Philip Marzo, Andrei
Koribanics
Client: A. Rodriguez

0362
Art Director: Philip Marzo
Designers: Philip Marzo, Dave Sailer
Client: Glenn Susser

0389
Art Director/Designer: Philip Marzo
Client: Harvest Restaurants

0546
Art Director/Designer: Philip Marzo
Client: Village Cellar

Richard Poulin Design Group
286 Spring St., Sixth Floor
New York, NY 10013
USA
212-929-5445

0069
Art Director/Designer: Richard Poulin
Client: Merchandise Mart Properties, Inc.

0639
Art Director/Designer: Richard Poulin
Client: United Nations Plaza Hotel
(Ambassador Grill)

0645
Art Director/Designer: Richard Poulin
Client: The Drake Hotel, New York City
(La Piazzetta)

Rickabaugh Graphics
384 West Johnstown Rd.
Gahanna, OH 43230
USA
614-337-2229

0396
Art Director/Designer: Barry Spector
Illustrator: Suzanne Ketchoyian
Client: Grace Restaurant Services
(Broadway Museum Café)

0438
Art Director: Eric Rickabaugh
Designer/Illustrator: Tina Zientarski
Client: Fritz & Alfredo's

Rome & Gold Creative
1606 Central Ave. SE, Suite 102
Albuquerque, NM 87106
505-897-0870
USA
www.rgcreative.com

0018, 0019, 0020, 0022, 0023, 0024
Art Director: Lorenzo Romero
Designer: Robert E. Goldie
Client: Boba Tea Company

0021
Art Director: Robert E. Goldie
Designer: Lorenzo Romero
Client: Solomon's Porch

0278, 0703
Art Director/Designer: Julie Hale
Client: Toulouse Café

0348
Art Director: Lorenzo Romero
Designer: Robert E. Goldie
Client: Boba Tea Company

0360
Art Director: Lorenzo Romero
Designers: Robert E. Goldie, Julie Hale
Client: World View Café

0509
Art Director: Lorenzo Romero
Designer: Robert E. Goldie
Client: Boba Tea Company

0510
Art Director: Robert E. Goldie
Designer: Lorenzo Romero
Client: Boba Tea Company

0704
Art Director: Lorenzo Romero
Designer: Robert E. Goldie
Client: Boba Tea Company

0705
Art Director: Lorenzo Romero
Designer: Robert E. Goldie
Client: Boba Tea Company

0768
Art Director: Lorenzo Romero
Designer: Robert E. Goldie
Client: Boba Tea Company

0799
Art Director: Lorenzo Romero
Designer: Robert E. Goldie
Client: Boba Tea Company

0837
Art Director: Lorenzo Romero
Designers: Zeke Sikelianos, Robert E. Goldie
Client: Boba Tea Company

0838, 0839, 0840, 0841
Art Director: Lorenzo Romero
Designers: Zeke Sikelianos, Robert E. Goldie
Client: Boba Tea Company

0873, 0874
Art Director: Robert E. Goldie
Designer: Lorenzo Romero
Client: Boba Tea Company

Rusty Kay & Associates
2665 Main St.
Suite F
Santa Monica, CA 90405
USA

0630
Art Director: Rusty Kay
Designer: Randall Momii
Photographer: Bill VanScoy
Client: Hurry Curry (Michael Bank, Randy La Ferr)

S&N Design
121 North Eighth St.
Manhattan, KS 66502
USA
785-539-3931
www.sndesign.net
info@sndesign.net

0127, 0628
Art Director/Designer: Steve Lee
Client: So Long Saloon

0296
Art Director/Designer: Steve Lee
Client: Cox Bros. Smoke House

0563, 0627, 0954
Art Director/Designer: Steve Lee
Client: Harry's

0620, 0715
Art Director: Steve Lee
Designers: Chris Barrett, Steve Lee
Client: CoCo Bolos

Sabin Design
13476 Ridley Rd.
San Diego, CA 92129
USA
619-484-8712

0649
Art Director: Linda Natal
Designer/Illustrator: Tracy Sabin
Client: Horton Plaza Farmer's Market and Buffet

Sagmeister Inc.
222 W. 14th St.
New York, NY 10011
USA

0584, 0890
Art Director/Designer: Stefan Sagmeister
Client: Green Street (Tony Goldman)

Sayles Graphic Design
3701 Beaver Ave.
Des Moines, IA 50310
USA
515-279-2922
www.saylesdesign.com

0172
Art Director/Designer/Illustrator: John Sayles
Client: Rich Murillo (Nacho Mammas)

0200
Art Director/Designer: John Sayles
Client: Bass Street Chop House

0217
Art Director/Designer: John Sayles
Client: Tonic

0287
Art Director/Designer: John Sayles
Client: Blue Ribbon Steakhouse

0288
Art Director/Designer: John Sayles
Client: Java-B-Good

0292
Art Director/Designer: John Sayles
Client: Perky Parrot

0295
Art Director/Designer: John Sayles
Client: Sauce

0631
Designer: John Sayles
Photographer: Bill Nellans
Client: Chelsea Restaurant and Bar (Westin Chicago)

0652
Designer: John Sayles
Photographer: Bill Nellans
Client: 801 Steak & Chop House

Schumaker
466 Green St.
San Francisco, CA 94133
USA
415-398-1060

0634
Art Director/Designer: Ward Schumaker
Client: Moose's

Sea Design
70 St. John St.
London EC1M 4DT
UK
+44 020 7566 3100
www.seadesign.co.uk

0001, 0002, 0003, 0074, 0107, 0179
Art Directors: John Simpson, Bryan
Edmondson
Client: OQO

Shamlian Advertising
128 Mansion Dr.
Media, PA 19063
USA

0665
Art Director: Fred Shamlian
Designer: Stephen Bagi
Illustrators: Heidi Stevens, Susan
Harvey, Ginger DiMaio
Photographers: Barry Halkin, Joe Farley
Client: Passerelle

sky design
50 Hurt Plaza, Suite 500
Atlanta, GA 30303
USA
404-688-4702
tvaught@at.asdnet.com

0041, 0042, 0126, 0906
Art Director: Thom Williams
Designer: W. Todd Vaught
Client: Toast

0134, 0135, 0699, 0698, 0729
Art Director: W. Todd Vaught
Designers: W. Todd Vaught, Carrie
Brown, Tiffany Chen
Client: Concentrics Restaurant Group

Smart Works
113 Ferrars St.
Southbank, Victoria 3006
Australia
+61 03 8699 1111
www.smartworks.com.au

0258, 0601, 0833, 0865, 0916
Art Director/Designer: Paul Smith
Client: Funk Fish Café

Spark Communications, Inc.
327 E. Maryland Ave.
Royal Oak, MI 48067
USA
248-545-9012
www.spark-communications.com

0307
Art Director/Designer: Sherri Lawton
Client: The Inn Place

Spark Studio Pty Ltd
11 Yarra St.
South Melbourne, Victoria, 3205
Australia
+61 3 9686 4703
www.sparkstudio.com.au
info@sparkstudio.com.au

0223, 0444, 0858, 0911
Art Director: Sean Pethick
Designer: Natalie Leys
Client: Three Below

Stanley Moskowitz Graphics
474 Upper Samsonville Rd.
Samsonville, NY 12476
USA
914-657-8974

0314
Art Director/Designer/Illustrator:
Stanley Moskowitz
Client: On Rye

Strata-Media, Inc.
3590 Harbor Gateway N
Costa Mesa, CA 92626
USA
714-460-1205
www.strata-media.com

0212
Art Director: Todd Henderson
Designers: Todd Henderson, Jason Simon
Client: Creme de la Creme

STRONGtype
91 Prospect St.
Dover, NJ 07802-1520
USA
973-919-4265
www.strongtype.com

0418
Art Director: Richard Puder
Client: Faregrounds Restaurant

Studio Output
2 Broadway
The Lace Market
NG1 1PS Nottingham
UK
+44 0 115 950 7116
www.studio-output.com
info@studio-output.com

0006, 0007, 0177, 0441, 0442
Designer: Rob Cole
Client: Tea Factory

0008, 0009, 0010, 0031, 0185
Art Director: Dan Moore
Designer: Lydia Lapinski
Client: Geisha

0079, 0083, 0175
Art Director/Designer: Steve Payne
Client: Brass Monkey

0176 , 0411
Art Director: Dan Moore
Designer: Sara Oakley
Photographer: Philip Watts
Client: Lizard Lounge

Studio Seireeni
708 South Orange Grove
Los Angeles, CA 90036
USA
213-937-0355

0257
Art Directors: Richard Seireeni, Romane
Cameron
Designer/Illustrator: Romane Cameron
Client: Fred's 62

Taxi Studio Ltd.
93 Princess Victoria St.
Clifton, Bristol BS8 4DD
UK
+44 0 117 973 51 51
www.taxistudio.co.uk

0098, 0099, 0233, 0401.
Art Director: Spencer Buck
Designer: Olly Guise
Client: Goldbrick House

TD2, Identity and Strategic Design
Ibsen 43, 8th Floor. Polanco
México D.F. 11 560
+52 55 5281 6999
www.td2.com.mx
contacto@td2.com.mx

0203
Art Director: Rafael Treviño
Designers: Rodrigo Córdova, Adalberto
Arenas, Mauricio Muñoz
Client: La Posada

0304
Art Directors: Rafael Treviño, Rodrigo
Córdova
Designer: José Luis Patiño
Client: Frankfurt Restaurant

0334
Art Director/Designer: Rodrigo Córdova
Client: Sutra

0335
Art Director: Rafael Treviño
Designers: Rodrigo Córdova, Gabriela
Zamora
Client: Yushan Restaurant

0336
Art Director: Rafael Treviño
Designers: Rodrigo Córdova, Mauricio
Muñoz
Client: Chin-ai

0753
Art Director: Rafael Treviño
Designers: Gabriela Zamora, Rodrigo
Córdova
Client: Paddock Café

Tharp Did It
50 University Ave.
Suite 21
Los Gatos, CA 95030
USA
408-354-6726

0148
Art Director: Rick Tharp
Designers: Rick Tharp, Jean Mogannam,
Jana Heer
Client: Le Boulanger Bakeries

0156
Client: Bakeries by the Bay (101 Bakery
Café)
Art Director: Rick Tharp
Designers: Rick Tharp, Jean Mogannam

Thielen Designs
115 Gold Ave., Suite 209
Albuquerque, NM 87104
USA
505-205-3157
www.thielendesigns.com

0313, 0322
Art Director/Designer: Tony Thielen
Client: Sunshine Café

0321
Art Director: Tony Thielen
Designers: Tony Thielen, Randy Heil
Client: Sunshine Café

Threefold
95 Green St.
Richmond
Melbourne, VIC 3121
Australia
+61 3 9421 8988
belinda@threefold.com.au

0298, 0443, 0718, 0857, 0861, 0921
Art Director/Designer: Pom Kimber
Illustrator: Tom Samek
Client: Vue de Monde

Tomato Košir S. P.
Britop 141
S1-4000 Kranj
Slovenia
+386 41 260 979
tomato@siol.net

0151
Art Director/Designer: Tomato Košir
Client: Sax Pub

Tom Varisco Designs
608 Baronne St.
New Orleans, LA 70113
USA
514-410-2888
www.tomvariscodesigns.com

0196
Art Director: Tom Varisco
Designers: Rebecca Carr, Jeff Louviere,
David Caruso
Client: Cochon

Turnstyle
2219 NW Market St.
Seattle, WA 98107
USA
206-297-7350
www.turnstylestudio.com

0195, 0740, 0820, 0917
Art Director: Ben Graham
Designers: Ben Graham, Steve Watson
Client: Matador Restaurant

Ultra Design
2454, Rua Padre
Anchieta
Curitiba PR 80730 000
Brazil
+55 (41) 3016 3023
www.ultradesign.com.br

0239, 0600, 0776
Art Director: Bráulio Carollo
Designer: Raul Ramos
Client: Roy Bean Burgers

0353, 0610
Art Director: Braulio Carollo
Designer: Raul Ramos
Client: Villa Marcolini

0354
Art Director/Designer: Braulio Carollo
Client: Marcolini Gelateria

Unreal
12 Dyott St.
London WC1A 1DE
UK
+44 0 20 7379 8752
www.unreal-uk.com

0181
Art Director: Brian Eagle
Designer: Copper Giles
Client: Sphere

0182
Art Director: Brian Eagle
Designer: Copper Giles
Client: Shake

0184
Art Director: Brian Eagle
Designer: M. R. Bragg
Client: Food Food

0381
Designer: M. R. Bragg
Client: The Cock & Trumpet

urban INFLUENCE design studio
423 Second Ave. Ext., South Suite 32
Seattle, WA 98104
USA
206-219-5599 x204
www.urbaninfluence.com

0152, 0187, 0717
Art Director/Designer: Henry Yiu
Client: Ticklefish

0186, 0926, 0927
Art Director: Henry Yiu
Designers: Michael Mates, Pete Wright,
Henry Yiu
Client: La Vita È Bella

0409
Art Director: Henry Yiu
Designers: Henry Yiu (folder), Ivona
Konarski, Henry Yiu (inside pages only)
Client: Queen City Grill

0410
Art Director: Henry Yiu
Designers: Henry Yiu (folder), Ivona
Konarski, Henry Yiu (inside pages only)
Client: Frontier Grill

Val Gene Associates
5208 Classen Blvd.
Oklahoma City, OK 73118
USA

0490, 0566, 0567, 0568
Art Director/Designer: Lacy Leverett
Production: Shirley Morrow
Photographer: Chuck Doswell III
Client: Eagle's Nest

0579, 0580
Art Director and Designer: Lacy
Leverett
Illustrator: Morrow Design, Shirley
Morrow
Client: Harry's American Grill & Bar

0581
Art Director: Lacy Leverett
Client: Pepperoni Grill

0597
Art Director/Designer: Lacy Leverett
Illustrator: Christopher Jennings
Production: Shirley Morrow
Client: Shorty Small's Great American
Restaurant

VINE360
9851 Harrison Rd. #320
Bloomington, MN 55437
USA
952-893-0504
www.VINE360.com
info@VINE360.com

0250
Designer: Joy Mac Donald
Client: Bittersweet

Vital Signs & Graphics
10 Timber Ln.
Ellington, CT 06029
USA
203-875-9745

0084, 0085, 0165
Art Director/Designer: Denise Fopiano
Benoit
Client: W.B. Cody's Bar-B-Que Grille

Vrontikis Design Office
2707 Westwood Blvd.
Los Angeles, CA 90064
USA
310-446-5446
www.35k.com

0114, 0122, 0228, 0275
Art Director/Designer: Petrula Vrontikis
Client: Global Dining, Inc.

0121, 0747, 0787, 0794
Art Director: Petrula Vrontikis
Designers: Petrula Vrontikis, Kim Sage
Client: Global Dining, Inc.

0330, 0710, 0716, 0991
Art Director: Petrula Vrontikis
Designers: Petrula Vrontikis, Lorna
Stovall (logo lettering), Trina Luong,
Deanna Thagard, Reagan Marshall
Client: Calistoga Bakery Café

0343, 0869
Art Director: Petrula Vrontikis
Designer: Katsu Nakamachi
Client: Global Dining, Inc.

0345
Art Director: Petrula Vrontikis
Designers: Petrula Vrontikis, May
Hartono
Client: Global Dining, Inc.

0373, 0821
Art Director: Petrula Vrontikis
Designer: Christina Hsaio
Client: Global Dining, Inc.

0659
Art Director: Petrula Vrontikis
Designer: Kim Sage
Client: Jacksons (Alan Jackson)

Walker Group
95 Morton St., 8th Floor
New York, NY 10014
USA
212-462-8000
www.wgcni.com

0054, 0071
Art Director: George Kewin
Designers: Ana Luisa Rolim, Brian Cuba,
Rob Lopez
Client: Pauli Moto's Asian Bistro

Warm Rain Ltd
67 Vyner St.
London E2 9DQ
UK
+44 020 8980 1984
www.warmrain.co.uk
studio@warmrain.co.uk

0066, 0691, 0692, 0693, 0694, 0733,
0782, 0800, 0928
Art Director: Mark Lawson Bell
Designers: Warm Rain Design Team
Client: Sketch

0280, 0863, 0864
Art Director: Mark Lawson Bell
Designers: Warm Rain Design Team
Client: Imli

0593, 0594, 0678, 0679, 0985
Art Director: Mark Lawson Bell
Designers: Warm Rain Design Team
Client: Sketch

0844, 0845, 0846, 0847
Art Director: Mark Lawson Bell
Designer: Murray Thompson
Client: Sketch

0848
Art Director: Mark Lawson Bell
Designers: Murray Thompson, Eva Simon
Client: Sketch

0849
Art Director: Mark Lawson Bell
Designers: Nina Zeigler, Jurgen Bey
Client: Sketch

0850
Art Director: Mark Lawson Bell
Designers: Murray Thompson, Jonathan
Stuart
Client: Sketch

Whitney-Edwards Design
14 West Dover St.
PO Box 2425
Easton, MD 21601
USA

0614
Art Director: Charlene
Whitney-Edwards
Designer: Barbi Christopher
Illustrator: Charlene
Whitney-Edwards
Client: Washington Street Pub

Willoughby Design Group
602 Westport Rd.
Kansas City, MO 64111
USA
816-561-4189
www.willoughbydesign.com

0011, 0013, 0017, 0025, 0551, 0695
Art Directors: Ann Willoughby, Zack
Shubkagel Designers: Stephanie Lee,
Brady Vest (Hammerpress)
Client: SPIN! Concepts (Gail Lozoff)

0014, 0015, 0016, 0549, 0706, 0822,
0823, 0974
Art Directors: Ann Willoughby, Zack
Shubkagel
Designers: Nate Hardin, Jessica
McEntire
Client: Sheridan's Lattés, Frozen
Custard

Wolken Communica
2562 Dexter Ave. N
Seattle, WA 98109
USA
206-545-1696
www.wolkencommunica.com

0237
Art Director: Kurt Wolken
Designers: Johann Gómez, Ryan
Burlinson
Client: Wonder Bar

XJR Design
700 N. Green St.
Chicago, IL 60622
USA
312-243-3377
www.wolkencommunica.com

0646
Art Director: Roger Foin
Designers: Roger Foin, Wilda Kemp
Illustrator: Leonardo da Vinci, with
alterations by the designers
Clients: Paul LoDuca, Kathy LoDuca
(Vinci)

ABOUT THE AUTHOR

Luke Herriott runs a UK-based design group called **Studio Ink**, specializing in design for print. As former design director of the international visual arts publisher Rotovision, he has worked with some of the world's leading creatives to produce a number of outstanding design publications.

With more than 15 years in the book publishing industry, he has a wealth of experience and an extensive knowledge of design, as well as a good awareness and appreciation of emerging graphic trends.

He is author of Rotovision's **The Packaging and Design Templates Sourcebook** and **The Designer's Packaging Bible** and co-author of **First Steps in Digital Design** and **Instant Graphics**.